"Many leaders have strong opinions about the advantages of remote work, but Raj Choudhury has something better: strong evidence. This book contains his pioneering research on how working from anywhere can be a competitive advantage. Ignore it at your own risk."

—**ADAM GRANT,** #1 *New York Times* bestselling author, *Think Again* and *Hidden Potential*; podcast host, *Re:Thinking*

"In this important and timely book, Choudhury lays out a blueprint for designing work in a more creative and humane way, delving into corporate practice to show what it takes in terms of culture, strategy, and leadership."

—**LYNDA GRATTON,** author, *The Shift*

"Choudhury is a leading voice on what the work-from-anywhere revolution means for cities and for nations. His expert insights come together in this timely, important, and well-researched book. It's a must-read for business leaders, policymakers, and anyone concerned with the future of work."

—**RICHARD FLORIDA,** bestselling author, *The Rise of the Creative Class*

"A visionary perspective on how embracing flexibility unlocks new levels of innovation and productivity. Choudhury reveals a compelling path for companies and professionals to transcend geographic limitations and achieve more in life and work."

—**HAYDEN BROWN,** President and CEO, Upwork

"Raj Choudhury is a renowned expert on remote work. In *The World Is Your Office*, he describes its various models and offers a road map for companies looking to work successfully in that environment."

—**SID SIJBRANDIJ,** cofounder and CEO, GitLab

"Choudhury's book is a timely and transformative source for leaders who want to create the flexible, inclusive, and productive workplaces of the future."

—**AMIR SALIHEFENDIC,** founder and CEO, Doist

"Choudhury brilliantly captures the essence of why work from anywhere isn't just a trend—it's the cornerstone of a more equitable and innovative future."

—**ANNIE DEAN,** Global Head, Team Anywhere, Atlassian

"I tap Raj Choudhury's seminal research and case studies on a regular basis with *Fortune* 500 executives. His book offers evidence of the benefits of workplace flexibility for firms, as well as practical advice for its frequent challenges, like collaborating across time zones and building connections that persist in distributed teams. Highly recommended reading for anyone looking to improve organizational performance or build thriving communities."

—**BRIAN ELLIOTT,** CEO, Work Forward;
cofounder and Executive Leader, Future Forum

"Choudhury's prodigious research coalesces in a new approach to managing workplaces and leading teams to improve access to talent and increase the chances that workers will thrive. Every organization can learn from the strategy and tactics he espouses."

—**KEVIN J. DELANEY,** cofounder, CEO, and Editor in Chief, Charter

"As someone who has been in the trenches of remote work for more than twenty years, I can confidently say that this book is a fantastic resource. It's a guide for anyone serious about building a sustainable and impactful distributed company."

—**LIAM MARTIN,** cofounder, Time Doctor; coauthor,
Wall Street Journal bestseller *Running Remote*

"Choudhury is making WFA plausible for more and more organizations."

—**DEBORAH LOVICH,** Managing Director and Senior Partner, Boston Consulting Group; fellow, Future of Work, BCG Henderson Institute

The World Is Your Office

PRITHWIRAJ CHOUDHURY

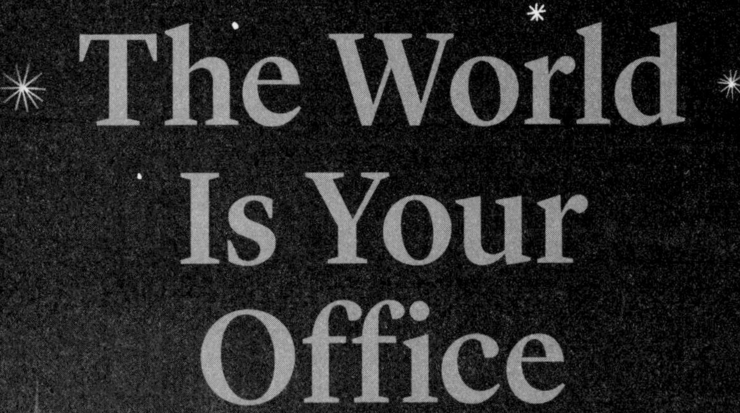

The World Is Your Office

How Work from Anywhere Boosts Talent, Productivity, and Innovation

HARVARD BUSINESS REVIEW PRESS
BOSTON, MASSACHUSETTS

HBR Press Quantity Sales Discounts

Harvard Business Review Press titles are available at significant quantity discounts when purchased in bulk for client gifts, sales promotions, and premiums. Special editions, including books with corporate logos, customized covers, and letters from the company or CEO printed in the front matter, as well as excerpts of existing books, can also be created in large quantities for special needs.

For details and discount information for both print and ebook formats, contact booksales@harvardbusiness.org, tel. 800-988-0886, or www.hbr.org/bulksales.

Copyright 2025 Prithwiraj Choudhury

All rights reserved

Printed in the United States of America

10 9 8 7 6 5 4 3 2 1

No part of this publication may be reproduced, stored in or introduced into a retrieval system, or transmitted, in any form, or by any means (electronic, mechanical, photocopying, recording, or otherwise), without the prior permission of the publisher. Requests for permission should be directed to permissions@harvardbusiness.org, or mailed to Permissions, Harvard Business School Publishing, 60 Harvard Way, Boston, Massachusetts 02163.

The web addresses referenced in this book were live and correct at the time of the book's publication but may be subject to change.

Library of Congress Cataloging-in-Publication Data

Names: Choudhury, Prithwiraj, author.
Title: The world is your office : how work from anywhere boosts talent, productivity, and innovation / Prithwiraj (Raj) Choudhury.
Description: Boston, Massachusetts : Harvard Business Review Press, [2025] | Includes index.
Identifiers: LCCN 2024035516 (print) | LCCN 2024035517 (ebook) | ISBN 9781647824716 (hardcover) | ISBN 9781647824723 (epub)
Subjects: LCSH: Telecommuting. | Flexible work arrangements. | Quality of work life.
Classification: LCC HD2336.3 .C46 2025 (print) | LCC HD2336.3 (ebook) | DDC 658.3/123--dc23/eng/20241213
LC record available at https://lccn.loc.gov/2024035516
LC ebook record available at https://lccn.loc.gov/2024035517

ISBN: 978-1-64782-471-6
eISBN: 978-1-64782-472-3

The paper used in this publication meets the requirements of the American National Standard for Permanence of Paper for Publications and Documents in Libraries and Archives Z39.48-1992.

To my parents,
Dr. Dhiraj Choudhury
and Gouri Choudhury

Contents

Introduction 1
Work from Anywhere, the Talent Strategy You've Been Looking For

PART ONE
Work from Anywhere: The New Talent Strategy

1 The Business Case for Work from Anywhere 15
2 Emerging WFA Trends 37

PART TWO
Managerial Strategies to Implement WFA

3 WFA and Communication 55
4 WFA and Knowledge Sharing 67
5 WFA and Isolation 81
6 Transitioning from Traditional Hybrid and WFH Models to WFA 103

Epilogue 119
WFA and the Future of the Workplace

Appendix A: Digital Nomad Visa Policies across Countries *123*
Appendix B: The Traditional Model for Relocating Talent: A Summary of the Research *127*
Notes *155*
Index *179*
Acknowledgments *189*
About the Author *191*

The World Is Your Office

Introduction

Work from Anywhere, the Talent Strategy You've Been Looking For

The world of work has changed. No longer is the downtown office the only performative stage for work. While the idea of remote work (a generic term used to describe work that is performed outside of the company office) and technologies to support distributed work arrangements (where workers are spread out across time zones and regions) have existed for decades, this book focuses on recent innovations in management practices.[1] Although the Covid-19 pandemic unleashed various forms of hybrid work, there is a more novel and highly desirable model of remote and distributed work, called work from anywhere (WFA), upending traditional and hybrid work arrangements alike.

WFA is a work arrangement that allows individuals to choose which cities, towns, or even countries they want to live in. Under

WFA, workers enjoy the flexibility to select their workspaces and work locations. They are awarded the freedom to work outside of the office if they so choose, and they can also opt to live anywhere, resulting in a distributed pattern for where workers reside. WFA is not the same as work from home (WFH) or a traditional hybrid work arrangement, in which workers may work occasionally outside of the physical office.

Why is WFA such an attractive proposition for workers and for companies? It gives individuals a better quality of life while enabling companies to hire diverse talent from around the world. In sum, work from anywhere enables companies to hire from anywhere.

The Game-Changing Talent Strategy

In a world where accessing high-quality talent is a source of competitive advantage, and where many postpandemic employees are predisposed to—and in some cases, demanding—remote and distributed work arrangements, WFA is a win-win for both companies and workers. To help organizations attract and retain diverse, high-quality talent from previously untapped talent markets, leaders and managers should consider WFA to be the most important talent strategy of the twenty-first century.

When implemented well, WFA can expand the talent pool accessible to both large and smaller organizations. If supported by the right management practices, workers across a wide variety of occupations—C-suite executives, accountants, finance professionals, lawyers, bankers, salespeople, technologists, marketing professionals, HR professionals, among others—can successfully adopt the WFA model. Indeed, in the foreseeable future, the company offsite might complement or even replace the downtown office as we know it. The WFA model may even move beyond traditional desk-based jobs; AI, machine learning, automation, and the digital twin revolution are extending the boundaries of WFA into blue-collar, semi-desk, and deskless worker settings, such as manufacturing, warehouses, hospital operations, airports, and even agriculture.

The World Is Your Office represents a decade of my research on WFA. It outlines several examples of successful WFA implementations. While in-person work was the past, and traditional hybrid appears to be the present . . . WFA is the future.

My Research

For more than a decade, as a management professor at Wharton and the Harvard Business School, I have studied the changing geography of work. Even prior to the pandemic, I made a business case for why companies should embrace WFA, and my belief in the benefits of WFA has been strengthened by the research I have conducted since then.[2] This research spans multiple continents—North America, South America, Europe, and Asia—and multiple industries—technology, financial services, manufacturing, utilities, and real estate—and it covers both established companies and startups. The study of WFA in the context of the United States Patent and Trademark Office that I led was cited in the 2022 Economic Report of the President of the United States. In

2023, *Forbes* recognized me in the Future of Work 50 list and in 2024, I was included in the Charter 30 list of leaders, thinkers, and innovators shaping the future of work.

I am writing this book now because business leaders need a clear strategic plan for why their companies should embrace WFA today. I also recognize that while WFA can unlock benefits for workers and companies alike, the successful implementation of WFA entails solving three problems: the communication problem, the knowledge-sharing problem, and the isolation problem. Implementing WFA boils down to effective management practices and leadership, and *I have the relevant experience of implementing change within firms.*

Prior to academia, I spent about a decade as a consultant with McKinsey & Company and working for technology firms such as Microsoft and IBM, with stints in Asia, Europe, and North America. In those roles I discovered two pertinent questions to be answered: What is the business case for WFA? And how do managers successfully implement WFA within a hybrid work plan? In this book, I answer both questions.

I also present my view of how the future of WFA is unfolding—for example, how automation, sensors, and AI are collectively expanding the reach of WFA into manufacturing, supply chain, hospitals, airports, agriculture, and other settings. Additionally, countries are competing for talent using digital nomad visa policies, and smaller towns around the world are attempting to reverse brain drain by leveraging WFA. *The World Is Your Office* makes the case that WFA must become part of a redesigned work arrangement. Change is hard. Don't settle for half the reward (a hybrid system that doesn't work for people and doesn't expand your access to talent) while investing in it; unlock the potential of work from anywhere.

The Way Forward

For business leaders considering a shift from a traditional WFH model that tethers employees to locations where the company has an office to WFA, there is likely to be some resistance from some senior managers, HR, legal, and even certain employees. But for every challenge or criticism of the WFA model, there are companies already working to establish a set of management practices to overcome them. Your company will be left behind, losing the talent game, if you don't think broadly about letting people work from anywhere. It is true that WFA might not be the right solution for every company or for every type of job, but I encourage each manager to set aside their preconceived notions of what *should* or *must* be done in person. If we start from a place of assuming that WFA is possible, it becomes a much more practical challenge to find the right combination of management practices that will make WFA work effectively for your team.

A Road Map for Navigating This Book

Whether you are an executive ready to move your company into the WFA future, or a manager in need of a compelling argument for why your leadership team should be open to exploring the world of WFA, this is the book for you. By the end, you will be able to articulate exactly what the benefits of work from anywhere are, understand the potential challenges associated with work from anywhere, and be equipped with a slate of policies and processes your company can put into place to make work from anywhere viable for your company. This doesn't mean that your organization will need to dive into the deep end of remote and distributed work and get rid of its office lease, but I offer the tools needed to expand everyone's comfort with WFA. With WFA policies in place, your company will be able to tap into new labor markets, attract and retain diverse workers, and potentially see improved worker satisfaction and productivity. And rather than being tied to a desk in a single building in one city, for you and your team, the world will be your office.

So where do we go from here? Chapter 1 presents the business case for WFA, emphasizing its importance as a means of hiring and retaining the best talent in your field. Chapter 2 introduces emerging trends in the world of WFA, specifically the digital nomad phenomenon and its accompanying shifts in global visa, benefit, and labor policies, and the ways that digital twin technologies are expanding the realm of the possible, moving previously in-person-grounded industries like utilities, farming, and manufacturing into the digital space (and therefore potentially into the scope of WFA).

The second part of the book considers the three key managerial challenges of WFA and presents policy solutions to those challenges. Chapter 3 focuses on communication, specifically the challenge of communicating across time zones, and the ways that asynchronous communication practices can mitigate this challenge. Chapter 4 reveals the knowledge-sharing problem—the task of globally distributed workers maintaining access to the information they need to do their jobs effectively in real time—and proposes documentation and handbook practices that can resolve the issue. Chapter 5 highlights the dual problem of professional and social isolation of remote workers, covering the learning and mentoring they need to advance in their careers, and the socialization opportunities required to foster a real sense of camaraderie and company culture from afar. This chapter makes the case for virtual watercoolers, offsites, and other thoughtfully structured chances for mentoring, learning, and socialization as a means of addressing these concerns. Chapter 6 looks at how to layer in WFA if your company has already embraced a hybrid work arrangement, with a step-by-step progression from a traditional hybrid organization to a WFA organization.

By the final chapter, you will find yourself well versed in how WFA fits into the changing geography of work, why your company would be better served by embracing work from anywhere, and how you should begin to implement these important changes in the way your company operates.

For those interested in the research underpinnings of my case for WFA and the growing popularity of hybrid work approaches, appendix B appears in the back of the book, highlighting the traditional relocation model of work-related mobility (in which firms historically hire from the talent pool where their offices are, or among workers willing to relocate), and the value created for workers and firms by accessing distant talent. This appendix also identifies challenges of this traditional relocation model—obstacles that can be overcome through the shift toward remote, distributed, and WFA arrangements. Also included is research into why hybrid work arrangements gained popularity and replaced in-person work so quickly. The answer lies in balancing two competing forces: flexibility and isolation. Striking the balance between these factors is key to determining what the ideal work arrangement for an organization might be.

A lot of terminology appears throughout this book in discussing various forms of remote work, distributed work, and working arrangements. For a quick reference to what each of these terms and acronyms means, see table I-1. You can return to it as you read if you need a reminder of what each working arrangement entails.

TABLE I-1

Summary of terms describing work arrangements

Term	Abbreviation	Definition
Remote work	Remote	Work that is performed outside the traditional company office. WFH and WFA are two different forms of remote work.
Work from home	WFH	Work that is performed outside the physical office, typically at home. WFH gives individuals flexibility on workspace.
Work from anywhere	WFA	Work that is performed outside the company office with employees choosing where to live, regardless of where the company is physically located. WFA gives individuals flexibility on *both* workspace and work location.
Hybrid work	Hybrid work	Work arrangement that allows workers to work remotely on certain days of the week or month.
Weekly hybrid (traditional hybrid)	W-Hybrid or traditional hybrid	Hybrid work arrangement where workers are required to be in-person one, two, three, or four days a week, with in-person days typically at the company office. Workers must live within commuting distance of their company's offices.
Monthly hybrid	M-Hybrid	Hybrid work arrangement where workers are required to be in-person one week every month. Teams are allowed to be flexible in deciding where to meet (in-person days could be at offsites, client sites, or even conferences).
Quarterly hybrid	Q-Hybrid	Hybrid work arrangement where workers are required to be in-person one week or longer every quarter. Teams are allowed to be flexible in deciding where to meet (in-person days could be at offsites, client sites, or even conferences).
All-remote or remote-first	All-remote	Work arrangement that allows all workers to work from anywhere. All-remote/remote-first companies often do not have any physical offices or have limited office space.
In-person	In-person	Work arrangement that allows no flexibility to workers on either workspace or work location. Workers work from a company office and live within commuting distance of the office.
Distributed work	Distributed	Work that is performed far away from colleagues. Given that WFA allows workers to choose where to live, WFA combines aspects of both remote work (i.e., working outside the office) and distributed work (i.e., living far away from colleagues).

Part One

Work from Anywhere: The New Talent Strategy

It is not enough to think of a future work arrangement in terms of simply allowing work from home (WFH)—in which workers may work occasionally outside the physical office—or traditional hybrid work—in which workers may work remotely more often but must remain within commuting distance of their company's offices—alone. We need to think of work from anywhere (WFA) as part of the future. Why should your company build its capacity to work from anywhere? Because to allow work from anywhere is to hire from anywhere. Accessing a national or even a global talent pool is a key advantage for companies that embrace WFA.

1

The Business Case for Work from Anywhere

For decades, an implied clause in employment contracts has been that the employer determines where employees get to live and set up home. The office has been the default performative stage for work, so millions of workers have packed up their lives and moved to the city, state, or country where their employer asked them to relocate. But relocation for work is a double-edged sword. While geographic mobility and in-person work offers several benefits, relocation also has several challenges (see appendix B for both benefits and challenges of relocation). So, what is to be done? What can a company do to access distant talent and reap the benefits of in-person work, while acknowledging and working to overcome the constraints of moving talent between locations?

I believe the most effective solution, for most companies, is to remove the need for permanent relocation altogether and embrace a work-from-anywhere (WFA) arrangement. Under a WFA arrangement, rather than needing to move workers to company locations, companies can move their work to where the talent is, giving workers the flexibility to relocate to their preferred geographic locations—or to *not* move if they are already in their preferred location. As I discuss in detail in chapter 5, an effective WFA model also entails occasional business trips to an office or an off-site location for the purposes of being colocated with team members and colleagues.

WFA, when conceived and implemented thoughtfully, can be a win-win-win—for companies, communities, and workers. Not only can a company position itself to better compete for distant talent if it offers WFA policies, but by removing geographic limits, businesses can expand their hiring pools to capture a more diverse set of talent worldwide. Work from anywhere opens new geographic labor markets for companies to access.

Research shows that WFA policies are associated with superior hiring outcomes and can result in increased worker productivity, lower employee turnover, and significant cost savings. In addition to these benefits and the ability to compete for global talent, WFA policies may also have positive societal effects, creating spillover benefits to workers' local communities. WFA can positively affect the lives of individual workers and their families in several ways.

Let's begin by exploring these benefits and review examples from my years of research with organizations that embraced and catalyzed WFA, like the United States Patent and Trademark Office (USPTO); startups such as Zapier, eXp, Doist, and MobSquad; global multinationals like TCS and GitLab; and nonprofits like the Tulsa Remote community program and BRAC.

Defining Work from Anywhere

WFA is simply a work arrangement that allows individual workers to decide where to live, regardless of where their employer's offices are located. Workers require a computer and a stable internet connection, but the choice of key variables related to the geography of work (work location, workspace, and work environment) is left up to them.

The state, city, or town where they live is entirely up to the employees. Whether they work from a company office, satellite office, home office, coworking space, coffee shop, or gym is left to their discretion. Consequently, workers can shape their choices of workspaces and work environments. They may select ambient silence or white noise, opt for outdoor versus indoor spaces, and can even tailor the temperature to their liking. There are some limits to these choices: The organization may specify the geographic landscape (the country, set of countries, state, or set of states, and even the time zones) where the worker may choose to live. For certain tasks, managers may require individuals to work from data-secure premises; they may mandate being present on camera at certain times of the week or require workers to attend team meetings in-person at a predetermined frequency and location. But broadly speaking, WFA shifts the game by allowing workers to decide where to live and work, rather than the company telling them where to relocate and live.

This granting of geographic flexibility to workers distinguishes WFA from other versions of remote work. Early versions of remote work—the type introduced well before the Covid-19 pandemic prompted a mass experiment with remote work—and specifically work-from-home (WFH) policies resulted in cutting down commute times for workers and allowed them to choose their workspaces and work environments. This form of remote work remains extremely popular in the post-Covid period and manifests as a version of a hybrid work embraced by many companies (more on this in chapter 6).

For some portion of the week, usually one or two days, workers operating under a traditional hybrid work arrangement can skip the daily commute and instead complete their work at home. WFH grants workers the flexibility to fully personalize their workspaces. When working from home, workers can spend more time outdoors, play with their kids, or take the dog for a walk while listening in on a team call or asynchronous work recording. This is in stark contrast to the traditional five-days-in-office model where workers had very little control over their work environments. Even details like the temperature of the office, or what can be displayed on their office walls, were decided by their employer. This is still true in swanky tech offices that provide snacks, beanbags, and massage chairs; with a few exceptions, workers are mostly working indoors in an environment controlled by the employer.

However, the work-from-home moniker hides the fact that under a WFH arrangement, individual workers *still remain tethered to locations where the firm has an office presence.* In other words, WFH offers less flexibility in work location (where employees live and work). While some workers can stretch the definition of "reasonable commuting distance" in choosing where to live, most workers remain contained within a commuting radius of where the company has preexisting offices. Theoretically, for workers required to come into the office one day per week, someone could spend every other week in a hotel to meet their in-office requirements. For most, however, WFH programs mandate that workers continue to live within an easy drive or train commute of their office. In other words, under a WFH arrangement, companies explicitly or implicitly decide where workers live and settle down.

The shift toward a WFA model—which began during the last decade but accelerated rapidly in response to the pandemic—introduces a great deal more control over geography for the worker. Rather than living at a location within easy commuting distance of the physical office—or creating convoluted workarounds to meet in-office requirements while living farther away—workers are granted the ability to select where to live and work. Many WFA companies still place limits on this ability, though, such as asking workers to reside within a specific time zone, or for those working on federal contracts, within the boundaries of the United States. WFA multinationals, too, implement some limits. For instance, if a company relies heavily on communication tools such as videoconferencing to function, countries like the UAE, where Zoom was banned until the government relaxed restrictions during the Covid-19 pandemic, weren't an option for their employees. But in general, WFA policies mean that workers have more flexibility in choosing where they want to live, compared to a traditional in-person work arrangement or a traditional hybrid arrangement. As in the case of WFH policies, WFA workers also continue to control their workspaces and environments. It is the freedom to control all three buckets—work location, workspace, and work environment—that I will use throughout this book to determine whether a company truly operates under a WFA model.

Table 1-1 summarizes the past, present, and future of work arrangements, distinguishing between flexibility in workspace (awarded by WFH) and flexibility in work location (awarded by WFA). The central premise here is that while in-person work represented the past, traditional hybrid work that incorporates days spent working from the office and working from home represents the present for most companies. WFA, which allows workers flexibility on both workspace and work location, is the future.

One compelling example of a successful WFA arrangement is modeled by the multinational firm GitLab. Founded in 2012, GitLab is a software as a service (SaaS) company that builds collaboration tools for distributed teams. Perhaps unsurprisingly, given

TABLE 1-1

The past, present, and future of work arrangements

Work arrangement	Description	Type of remote work and flexibility
In-person	Workers are mandated to work in a company office.	None
Traditional hybrid*	Workers are mandated to work in a company office for a few days every week and have to live within commuting distance of the office. Workers can work from home but cannot work from anywhere.	Flexibility to choose workspaces and work from home
WFA	There is no mandate to work at or live near a company office, and workers can work from anywhere.	Flexibility on both workspace and work location, i.e., work from anywhere

* Traditional hybrid can be also characterized as weekly hybrid. There are other forms of hybrid work arrangements (such as monthly hybrid and quarterly hybrid) that allow for WFA. See chapter 6 for more details.

the company's product, GitLab itself is distributed, with its more than two thousand employees spread across sixty-five countries worldwide. In fact, GitLab operates under one of the most extreme forms of remote work—all-remote—that eschews a physical office altogether. GitLab debuted as a public company in 2021, with a $7.7 billion valuation. Since then, the company has continued to grow, and it closed out 2023 with a valuation of $9.8 billion—as clear a sign as any that a company can not only survive but thrive while operating under a WFA model.[1]

Ultimately, embracing WFA policies will help companies both large and small compete in the global talent market, because many top-tier workers are actively searching out WFA roles. Particularly following the remote work revolution during the pandemic, one recent survey found that among workers who *could* work remotely, nearly one third would *prefer* to work remotely full-time.[2] In 2023, *Time* magazine reported on another survey claiming that companies offering WFA were hiring more quickly.[3] That survey found that between June 2022 and May 2023 companies requiring zero days in an office saw their headcount grow by 5.6 percent. In contrast, headcount increased by 3.8 percent for companies requiring employees to be in the office four days a week, and just 2.6 percent for those requiring workers to be on-site five days a week.[4] The evidence is equally compelling when viewed from the perspective of the traditional office in the downtown area or from the perspective of recent return-to-office (RTO) mandates. NYU Stern professor Arpit Gupta and colleagues estimate value destruction of more than $400 billion in the commercial real estate sector related to office buildings in the United States, due to large drops in lease revenues, occupancy, lease renewal rates, and market rents in the commercial office sector, precipitated by remote work.[5] Recent research also documents the donut effect, the hollowing out of work from the downtown region to peripheral suburbs across cities.[6] Another recent working paper using a sample of S&P 500 firms reports significant declines in employees' job satisfaction but no significant changes in financial performance or firm values after top-down return-to-office (RTO) mandates.[7]

Accessing Diverse Global Talent

One unique benefit of WFA policies is that organizations are enabled to hire from anywhere while attracting and retaining a diverse set of employees, wherever they are located. This aspect of WFA helps both large and small companies, but especially all-remote startups that do not have physical offices and as a result, don't need to compete with larger companies for talent exclusively located within clusters (in, for example, Bangalore or Silicon Valley). Recent research by Wharton's David H. Hsu and Prasanna B. Tambe validates this claim. The authors analyzed job applicant data from a leading startup job platform and reported that discrete changes in job posting to remote status (holding all else constant) are associated with an approximately 15 percent increase in applicants who are female, 33 percent increase in applicants with underrepresented minority status, and 17 percent increase in applicant experience.[8]

Several years ago, I was made aware of this particular benefit of WFA while studying all-remote companies such as eXp, Doist,

GitLab, and Zapier. All-remote organizations do not have physical offices and hire talent globally. Each employee, from interns to the CXO, works from anywhere. Sid Sijbrandij, cofounder and CEO at GitLab, described the evolution of how GitLab became all-remote. The company tried to lease offices several times, but each time ultimately gave up the leases when they realized that folks were not traveling to the offices and workers often preferred to live way beyond the commuting distance to any office. Sid had a robot named Beamy who circulated all day within an empty boardroom in San Francisco, broadcasting his video feed online to show that GitLab did *not* have people working in offices.

During my interviews, multiple founders of all-remote startups, including Sid at GitLab, Wade Foster at Zapier, and Amir Salihefendic at Doist, among others, admitted that a key advantage of the WFA model was the ability to hire diverse talent from faraway global locations that were brimming with underutilized talent. The traditional model of startups for decades was being located within large clusters such as Bangalore, London, Shanghai, Silicon Valley, Singapore, or Tokyo, and entailed competing with global multinationals for the talent that lived within these clusters. By eschewing physical offices and going all-remote, the founders of all-remote startups could now hire globally. Zapier, for example, has over eight hundred employees across thirty-eight countries.

My research on the all-remote organization eXp, with colleague and finance professor Jan Bena (at the University of British Columbia) also revealed another important incentive for why startup founders were attracted to the all-remote WFA model: the early absence of real estate and lease costs resulted in a leaner balance sheet and ensured that the founders retained greater equity during IPO.

The ability to hire from anywhere in a WFA model also benefits larger, more traditional companies. My research with the United States Patent and Trademark Office (USPTO) revealed that the switch to WFA (from WFH) allowed the USPTO to hire from colleges in the Western and Southern parts of the United States. As a senior manager at the USPTO told me, "We were struggling to hire software patent examiners, who were mostly living in California, and they would *not* relocate to Alexandria, Virginia, to work on federal wages. WFA opened several geographic talent pools for the USPTO."

Additionally, global technology giant Tata Consultancy Services (TCS) cited the ability to access a global talent pool as one of the key reasons it was considering a WFA model (in 2020, the company announced plans to be 75 percent remote within five years).[9] TCS is headquartered in India, and its more than four hundred thousand employees have historically worked in person at TCS or client offices. During my research with TCS, conducted in 2020–2021, the organization's former CEO and former COO revealed that the company was planning to move *closer* to a WFA model, only requiring workers to physically work from a company office for 25 percent of their workdays. At the time, leaders believed this change would allow TCS employees to live where they wanted to while working on more than one project. As an example, a TCS engineer could now live in her hometown in Kerala, India, and virtually work on two projects: one with a pharmaceutical client in New Jersey and another with a banking client in London. N. G. Subramaniam, the former COO of TCS, shared his hope that embracing WFA would help TCS tap into talent pools, like Eastern Europe, without having to invest in opening new physical offices in those regions. At the time of finalizing this book, TCS reported a leadership change and a shift in its remote work plans. However, I believe that the insights uncovered by this research continues to stand for larger organizations.

Workers may be unable or unwilling to move geographically for several reasons. Some key concerns might be visa restrictions, occupational licensing challenges, family obligations, or the financial and emotional costs of relocating. WFA policies allow companies to access talent that is unable or unwilling to relocate. Already, there is a cottage industry of organizations seeking to tap into this source of talent. The federal government has an entire class of overseas roles intended for the trailing spouses of diplomatic and military personnel.[10] With Professor William Kerr at the Harvard Business School, I conducted research with a Canadian company called MobSquad, which works with engineers employed at companies in the United States who are facing visa challenges.[11] MobSquad uses coworking spaces throughout Canada as satellite offices for US-based startups, and in doing so, helps employees get work and bypass the tedious US immigration and visa system. MobSquad works with Canada's Global Talent Stream to secure fast-tracked work permits, allowing employees to work and live in Canada, while American startups that need the talent can fill positions. Other companies that realized the value of WFA in arbitraging global talent include Andela, a startup helping connect African talent with global companies.[12]

Hiring data is also beginning to support the theory that remote hiring can create a more diverse applicant pool. In a 2022 report,

Meta found that shifting to remote hiring prompted an increase in US hires of Black, Hispanic, Native American, Alaskan Native, Pacific Islander, veterans, and/or people with disabilities, as well as an increase in global hires of women.[13] LinkedIn, meanwhile, found that, based on self-identifying data from job applicants, applications for remote jobs submitted by Black, Latino, and female applicants surged between 2019 and 2022, suggesting significant demand for remote work among historically underrepresented populations. This data revealed greater diversity in hiring patterns as well, as LinkedIn reported a 24 percent increase in Black workers, a 10 percent increase in female workers, and a 5 percent increase in Latino workers accepting remote job offers during this period.[14] In ongoing research, Suhani Jalota, a doctoral student at Stanford, and Lisa Ho, a doctoral student at MIT, document that remote work can create employment opportunities for women in countries and communities where the social and religious norms are stacked against women working outside of the home.[15]

Boosting Worker Productivity

When considering the business case for any new operating model, another question that managers should ask is: Will implementing this model improve productivity and profitability? In the case of WFA, the emerging evidence is positive, according to results of research I conducted with Cirrus Foroughi and Barbara Larson at the USPTO.

In 2006, the USPTO introduced a telecommuting (WFH) program for patent examiners. Then in 2012, it launched a WFA program, starting with a pilot that was open only to patent examiners already in the telecommuting program who had two years of experience working for the USPTO. We were able to analyze data on these patent examiners at three stages—in-office, working from home, and working from anywhere—and tracked how their productivity changed as they moved from WFH to WFA (as shown in figure 1-1). It helps that the job of a patent examiner lends itself to clear productivity metrics. Among other metrics, the USPTO uses the number of cases handled every week as a measure of productivity, something that researchers can observe. As an empirical social scientist, I also deeply care about parsing causality from

FIGURE 1-1

Predicted output (total actions) for patent examiners before and after starting a WFA pilot, by month

The gray area indicates the range of predicted output for this time period with 95% confidence.

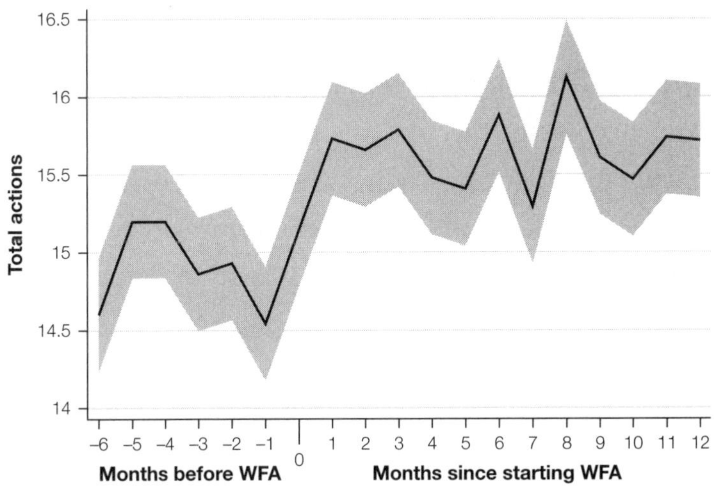

Source: Prithwiraj Choudhury, Cirrus Foroughi, and Barbara Larson, "Work-from-Anywhere: The Productivity Effects of Geographic Flexibility," *Strategic Management Journal* 42, no. 4 (2021): 655–683.

correlational patterns and at the USPTO, we were presented with a natural experiment to determine whether WFA indeed *caused* an increase in the number of cases handled. The union of patent examiners negotiated a monthly quota for how many patent examiners could transition from the traditional WFH program to the WFA program, and we established that the timing of transition was random. Given this natural experiment, we concluded that the transition from WFH to WFA resulted in a 4.4 percent increase in productivity, an increase that was over and above the productivity boost first seen when workers transitioned from a five-day, in-office model to WFH. We also found that the quality of patent prosecution did not change.

In addition to being more productive, workers under the WFA model may also have higher retention rates than their in-office counterparts. A year after rolling out their WFA program, we found that WFA resulted in higher retention, and the USPTO was voted the top agency to work for in an annual survey of federal workers.[16] Executives at GitLab, meanwhile, cite its all-remote model as one of the driving incentives for employee retention.

So why do we see these two patterns (enhanced productivity and higher retention rates) in response to WFA policies? Because WFA policies—specifically the geographic flexibility granted to workers under these policies—are valuable to the workers who were previously mandated to live in suboptimal work locations. For workers seeking out this flexibility in work location, they may now relocate to a place that enhances their quality of life.

Relocating to cheaper towns and receiving a boost to real income may be a draw for workers, particularly at companies that do not adjust salary by geographic location. At the USPTO, for example, workers are required to work in the USPTO offices in Virginia for two years before they begin working remotely, but at that point they can move anywhere in the United States and retain the same salary and benefits. Not only do many examiners choose to move to lower cost-of-living locations, but some of the workers indicate they specifically take the patent examiner job *because of this benefit*. Explained one examiner: "Some applicants take a job with us, come to headquarters, and they say, 'Okay, I can stick it out for two or three years in Alexandria, and I can move back home once I meet the requirements for TEAPP [Telework Enhancement Act Pilot Program] and work remotely.' So, we have a lot of people that do that. They just rent a place here for a couple years and then they go back to where they are from."[17] Another patent examiner shared that relocating to a cheaper town helped her enroll her children in childcare for the first time. In fact, my research with Thomaz Teodorovicz (Copenhagen Business School) and Evan Starr (University of Maryland) revealed that remote workers relocating to Tulsa (a relatively small city in Oklahoma), on average, experienced a lower cost of living and an increase in real income when their companies allowed them to participate in WFA.[18] One of the workers we interviewed told us, "I never thought I would own a house. Now I have two houses. I can also afford additional expenses for my children, like soccer practice and swimming."

The cost savings experienced by workers who work from anywhere prompts the debate on whether companies should adjust wages if workers relocate to cheaper towns. It might be tempting to adjust salaries if workers relocate to cheaper locations, but economics has long argued that workers should be compensated for their marginal productivity; and workers who work from anywhere are likely to be more, not less, productive than counterparts who do not enjoy geographic flexibility. While the evidence on adjusting wages (or not) is still out, in my opinion, companies should consider location-independent wages given that it makes economic sense, especially for jobs that are supply-constrained.

Beyond the lower cost of living, workers might enjoy a better quality of life when they are allowed to work from anywhere. In the USPTO setting, we found that older workers are more likely to relocate to Florida (think "Sunshine State of Work") and are more productive when they relocate from Virginia. Another individual relocating to Philadelphia shared that it enabled his family to access cutting-edge medical treatment for his daughter. In all cases, workers told me how grateful they were for their organization letting them choose where to live. In other words, WFA might enhance employee satisfaction and loyalty, and this could explain why they are more likely to be more productive while working from anywhere and remain in their jobs longer.

However, this all has a crucial boundary condition. The increase in effort and reduction in turnover applies only to workers who opt in to WFA, and who place a premium on the flexibility offered by WFA policies. In research at a Chinese travel agency, Stanford professor and remote work expert Nicholas Bloom and colleagues sought to quantify the productivity effects of a WFH model, and they found a clear association between workers *choosing* to participate in a remote work model and their productivity.[19] Their data is based on a group of workers who initially opted in to a WFH policy, and they found that in the initial six-month period of WFH, those workers experienced a productivity increase of 13 percent. However, when those workers were then asked whether they wanted to continue to work remotely, the workers who opted in for a second time saw an even larger jump in productivity of 22 percent. This reveals that for workers who value flexibility after experiencing it and have a clear understanding of its benefits and challenges, the combination of better work location and additional effort put forth means they are likely to be more productive workers when able to work under a WFA model.

It is important to note here that the challenges of remote work are real and significant. Ongoing academic research also points out that remote work in some settings can hurt productivity. In a recent paper, Natalia Emanuel at the Federal Reserve Bank of New York and Emma Harrington at the University of Virginia document that at a *Fortune* 500 call center, remote work degraded call quality—particularly for inexperienced workers—and reduced workers' promotion rates.[20] Issues like isolation, ineffective communication, and lower likelihood of career progression are particularly relevant to the discussion of how WFA relates to worker productivity and attrition. These topics will be covered in greater detail in part two, which lays out the challenges of WFA and managerial strategies for successfully implementing a WFA model.

Cost Savings Associated with WFA

The WFA model can also generate significant cost savings for companies that implement these policies. Fixed costs associated with maintaining physical office space, including real estate, utilities, and equipment costs, can be reduced. This seems like common sense: Apple famously spent $5 billion and eight years constructing its Silicon Valley headquarters.[21] The campus is spread over sixty-four acres and is designed to house twelve thousand employees. That's more than $416,000 spent per employee. If the company were fully remote, it could have given each worker a stipend to set up a home office and still seen massive savings. For an accurate figure, the savings would need to be amortized over the lifetime of the campus, but it is clearly a hefty budget line item for companies with traditional in-office work models.

For companies that implemented WFA policies and reduced (or eliminated) their physical office spaces, these savings are not theoretical. In 2015, the USPTO calculated an estimated savings of nearly $39 million due to increased remote work.[22] A study by Global Workplace Analytics revealed that remote work saved IBM and Sun Microsystems $50 million and $68 million, respectively, on real estate.[23] GitLab estimates that having an all-remote workforce saves them nearly $18,000 per year, per employee.[24] In fact, companies should consider reinvesting some of these savings to organize offsites for employees to meet in person (something I discuss further in chapter 6). But remember, the ability to attract and retain diverse and productive talent is the raison d'être for implementing WFA, not cost savings.

Harnessing Societal Benefits

Another consideration for businesses curious about whether to implement a WFA model is its macro scale effects: How can WFA policies within one business have spillover benefits to the communities where WFA workers live and where WFA businesses operate? On this broader scale, WFA policies do offer some clear advantages, including the environmental impacts of reducing or eliminating commutes, and the societal benefits of remote workers moving to areas suffering from brain drain.

As American commutes grow longer and longer, and remain mostly reliant on cars, the environmental pollution generated by the average commute is estimated to be 3.2 tons annually.[25] Though it is hoped that the emergence of electric vehicles and expansion of transit options will bring these rates down over time, WFA policies provide an immediate way to reduce individual emissions. In 2018, the USPTO sought to quantify the pollution reductions that resulted from its WFA program and found that in 2015 (three years after implementing WFA), the agency estimated that its remote workers avoided driving 84 million miles, thus reducing emissions by more than forty-four thousand tons.[26]

Looking at societal benefits, many smaller cities and towns as well as rural areas suffer from brain drain, when highly skilled or talented individuals migrate in search of a better standard of living. Residents seeking higher education or exceptionally skilled and high-paying jobs are unable to find them in the areas where they grew up, and so move to cities and urban centers like Silicon Valley and the BosWash corridor in the Northeast. The net result of this brain drain is an unequal spatial distribution of talent and jobs. Areas suffering from brain drain can struggle to retain or attract a diverse range of professionals or companies that might create the desirable jobs. There are talent attraction programs in place that seek to address this problem, such as immigration initiatives that fast-track residencies for doctors willing to live in regions that lack sufficient medical professionals, or the Teach for America program that sends college graduates to teach in underserved areas.[27] But these talent attraction programs arguably do not solve the chicken-and-egg problem for smaller towns—with talent leaving, companies are hesitant to set up offices, and the lack of companies and jobs precipitates greater brain drain. WFA can possibly break this vicious cycle as remote workers relocate to smaller towns without the need for being employed locally. The rise of WFA has prompted several regions in the United States, notably in Hawaii, Vermont, West Virginia, Northwest Arkansas, Topeka, Kansas, and the Shoals, Alabama, to create programs to attract remote workers who can work from anywhere.

In Tulsa, Oklahoma, for instance, the Tulsa Remote program offers remote worker participants $10,000 to relocate to Tulsa and live there for a year.[28] Among the core tenets of the program: participants must be remote workers prior to relocating and need to engage with or volunteer in the Tulsa community in some capacity. Since the program began in 2018, more than twenty-five hundred people (program participants and family) have relocated to Tulsa. Many of them have purchased homes and integrated into the local community, and they say they intend to settle in the area permanently. In research with Teodorovicz and Starr, I surveyed WFA workers who relocated to Tulsa and workers who were selected to relocate but either had not moved or had not yet moved and found that those who moved reported a greater number of hours spent in community volunteering programs, benefiting the local community in Tulsa. One of the Tulsa "remoters" I interviewed was a Black man who relocated from New York and now volunteers with the local high school as a debate coach, the first person of color in that position. Individuals also revealed in interviews why they were able to contribute more to community efforts in Tulsa (compared to when they lived in New York or other large cities): Tulsa was a smaller city, and it took less time to commute to volunteering projects!

By attracting workers with preexisting remote jobs who have a stated intention to engage deeply in their new city, Tulsa Remote arguably helps offset the ill effects of brain drain that has plagued Middle America for decades, fuels the city's housing, talent, and volunteer ecosystems, and has created a template for other smaller cities and regions around the world that are losing talent. I say this, however, with a word of caution. WFA has triggered a digital nomad migration revolution, so cities and communities will need to think carefully about how to manage their talent attraction programs in a way that will maximize the benefits from the presence of WFA migrants, while mitigating concerns around gentrification and cost-of-living increases.

As with any management policy, whether WFA will be successful will depend on *how* exactly your company decides to implement these policies; like any other management practice, WFA can be implemented well or poorly. But for managers considering whether to implement a WFA model at their firm, it is clear that WFA policies come with important benefits. WFA can allow your company to expand access to and tap into new geographic pools of talent, increase worker productivity, improve worker retention, save on real estate and other costs, and potentially have secondary positive effects on your local environment and community.

2

Emerging WFA Trends

To tap into global talent, companies and managers need to embrace WFA. And while it might be easy for leaders to dismiss WFA as relevant only to technology companies and other startups, they would be wrong. In fact, with a combination of sensors, automation, cloud technologies, and AI, WFA is primed to expand into any number of new industries. Meanwhile, WFA workers and companies are also broadening their horizons, exploring new work locations and defining more of the policies needed to run a truly global firm.

In this chapter we examine some of the emerging trends and future directions that WFA—and remote work more broadly—might take: First is the proliferation of digital twin technologies, which allow physical operations to be monitored and managed virtually. By mapping these operations in real time to the virtual world, digital twins make it possible for the frontiers of WFA to expand into jobs and industries where it was previously impossible. Once a manufacturing plant, hospital, or warehouse can be controlled from a kitchen table, or an agricultural field can be weeded from a home office, the bounds of what jobs can be done remotely have to be rethought completely. The second trend is the expansion of remote work and WFA with its attendant emerging policy implications, particularly in regard to taxation, social welfare programming, and other place-specific benefits. And finally is the explosion of digital nomads: remote workers who travel abroad for extended or finite periods and may even move from one country to another as they work remotely. Countries around the world seeking to compete for these workers are rolling out visa programs, tax exemptions, and other incentives to bring digital nomads to their shores.

Digital Twins Open the Door to WFA in More Industries

To date, most of the discussions surrounding remote work and WFA have centered on traditional white-collar, desk-based jobs—occupations like computer programming, IT help desks, accounting, legal, marketing, HR, and editorial services. Technological advances, specifically the expansion of the use of digital twin technology, are creating opportunities for more tasks and jobs to be performed remotely using digital tools. In turn, these opportunities present vast possibilities for sectors traditionally seen as in-person workplaces—like agriculture, manufacturing, and warehouse operations—to become welcoming of WFA.

Digital twin technology is an umbrella term used to describe the process of replicating a real-world operation in real time but done so using a digital format. One simple example is a control center in a factory. Rather than needing to stand next to a machine to read its settings, a digital twin would allow the worker to monitor (and often, control) the settings via a digital and virtual dashboard. The worker might be sitting in an office, or even at home, to monitor and control the functions of the dashboard. Digital twins can go beyond reporting and allowing access to simple settings. When combined with machine learning algorithms, digital twins can even begin to make operational adjustments autonomously.

Applications of digital twin technology are at work in a range of industries, including agriculture, transportation, health care, and manufacturing. In farming, digital twins are being used to monitor and care for agricultural crops from afar.[1] With time, these processes could also become automated, with an algorithm deciding when to weed or water a field based on the reports from the field's digital twin. At Rome's international airports, digital twin technologies have been used to develop a dashboard tracking passenger flows through the facility.[2] This dashboard allows the airport operations center to react in real time to events like flight delays, which can have cascading effects from requiring later flights to change their scheduled gates of arrival/departure to adjusting staffing levels at security, immigration, and baggage areas. Through a partnership with Siemens, Dublin's Mater Private Hospital developed a digital twin of its radiology department, allowing it to visualize and track its MRI and CT workflows to improve the patient experience.[3] As a result, the hospital ultimately reorganized the department layout and improved patient wait times and other key metrics. Finally, BMW is developing smart factories, starting with a facility in Hungary slated to open in 2025.[4] BMW engineering teams will be able to control every aspect of the production lines at the facility virtually, reducing the time between design, testing, and physical production.

The introduction of these digital twin technologies can be beneficial to workers, allowing them greater geographic flexibility, though of course, as digital twins lead to increasing automation of tasks, there is necessarily some displacement and/or reskilling of workers. I am currently studying the digital twin model at the Turkish energy company Enerjisa Üretim. The company has created a digital twin headquarters in Istanbul, centralizing all operations in a single room, overseeing multiple power plants across Turkey. Working in the digital twin headquarters enables the engineers at this company to live in Istanbul, instead of a remote region of Turkey.

But this rearrangement of work has also required engineers to be upskilled and reskilled in areas such as machine learning, visualization of data, and so forth. I strongly feel that the emergence of digital twins and the adoption of WFA in deskless settings will create a genre of so-called sky-blue-collared workers, workers at the intersection of blue-collar and white-collar work. Such workers will be skilled in operating and fixing expensive machinery but will also be capable of manipulating, visualizing, and interpreting data. (See figure 2-1.) This upside of digital twin technology is particularly relevant for jobs that have traditionally required the presence of human workers in unsafe and faraway places, like mining and on offshore oil rigs. Doing these tasks remotely, even if just from a nearby office, reduces the chance of injury on the job and a better work-life balance. Furthermore, once a digital twin allows operations to be monitored from a distance, what is to stop

FIGURE 2-1

The benefits of digital twins as workers move to WFA

Digital twin technology allows workers to visualize, manipulate, and interpret data from far-flung operations.

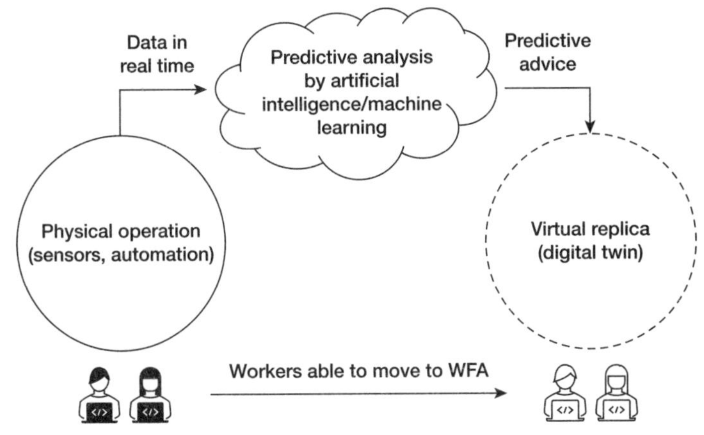

that distance between the worker and the operation from increasing exponentially? If a production line can be run from the plant manager's kitchen table, why couldn't it also be run by someone half a world away?

This geographic flexibility opens a lot of doors, particularly for global companies overseeing production in many countries. One example of this is Unilever, which I studied during the rollout of its digital twin technology in a Brazilian factory manufacturing detergents.[5] There, the company combined digital twins of every machine in the factory with data processing and AI tools to not only move control of the machines to a centralized dashboard, but also to automate many of the adjustments traditionally done by a machine operator (for instance, adjusting controls related to how much gas was to be used to dry the detergents, according to the temperature and humidity levels in the factory). These changes allowed the company to optimize its processes, manufacturing larger quantities faster and reducing consumption of gas. They also changed the staffing requirements of the factory, both in terms of the total number of operators needed, either onsite or virtually, and the type of experience required for the factory workers (machinists versus engineers). Though the need to retrain or downsize its operational staff proved to be a major challenge for Unilever, overall, the benefits of digitization and virtual operations were clear. Since then, the company has digitized more factories worldwide, in Indonesia, South Africa, and elsewhere, and has been toying with the idea of opening a global operations center to oversee its global production.

This model could be extended to different companies and industries with a digital twin center being located where workers want to live, allowing them to enjoy the benefits of geographic flexibility. Digital twin technology can ultimately extend the opportunity of WFA to all kinds of new industries, tasks, and frontline and deskless workers in factories, warehouses, farms, hospitals, airports, and power plants, among other settings.

Implementing digital twins requires a strategic plan focused on upskilling, reskilling, and retrenchment of workers. As I discussed in the Turkish case study, upskilling is the process of learning new skills to optimize the performance of a worker in their area of expertise, working with a piece of machinery or equipment; the advanced skills could be in areas such as electrical engineering, mechanical engineering, hydraulics, or data science. Reskilling is the process of learning new skills to prepare a worker for a different function, such as transitioning a worker from being a hydroelectric power plant operator to interpreting data and machine learning algorithms while working at the digital twin headquarters. Enerjisa Üretim created a one-year program to upskill and reskill workers and set up an in-house institute to provide both in-classroom and experiential training.

In the case of Unilever, the digital twin implementation required upskilling workers from being basic operators to becoming technical operators, and this transition often required a three-year certification at most locations. A typical basic operator in Unilever's Brazilian factory could perform tasks such as adjusting bottles of product to make sure they faced the same way, fastening the lids of jars after they were filled, or filling the bottle or cap hopper at the start of the line. On the other hand, technical operators manipulated machinery on an automated production line and could investigate minor issues and, if needed, make repairs. The company also helped transition its manufacturing workforce into new roles within the factory or at other locations within the company (such as desk-based jobs in offices) and helped workers find new careers through online learning and entrepreneurship training. In the Unilever factory at Indaiatuba, Brazil, a technology lab was set up to offer training to factory workers using software such as Jupyter Notebook for data analysis and Azure for cloud storage, so that they could explore skills to hone and careers to pursue.

Shifting National and Regional Policies to Accommodate WFA

Another question that must be addressed as WFA proliferates across companies is what policy changes are needed related to immigration, taxation, social security, and other state benefits.

Many of these policies hinge on the geographical place of employment and residence; for those who no longer live and work in the same place, or for those who split time across multiple places, this factor can be a major complication.

In the European Union, member states are in an ongoing discussion about how remote work and WFA should affect their policies. Historically, spending 75 percent of an individual's time in any one EU country was a good barometer for whether that country was the individual's place of residence. However, a more geographically mobile workforce could affect that characterization.[6] Furthermore, a worker's place of residence can also have major implications for benefits and entitlements. Different countries have wildly varying standards when it comes to issues like mandated leave requirements, contract clauses, and even the timelines for termination. Juggling these policy differences can be a major challenge for a company with a growing remote workforce, particularly if the organization does not already have offices in multiple regions of the world.

For companies allowing their workers to work from anywhere, understanding the variation in these policies across countries and regions is key to effective implementation of WFA. While running astray of these regulations certainly can have consequences for the individual workers, many of these laws may also have negative effects for companies found to be out of compliance. For instance, the question of where an employee's permanent residence lies can have implications for whether a company must have a legal entity in that country, and whether the company must pay corporate tax there. In the United Kingdom, for example, the state continues to grapple with how workers splitting their time would or wouldn't fall under the auspices of "permanent establishment"—the metric for determining whether individuals or businesses have enough of a presence in the United Kingdom to trigger tax obligations and access to local benefits. Their guidance suggests that even when split among multiple workers, if a foreign company had an ongoing presence in the country, it could be enough to establish a permanent foothold for the company under British law.[7] For example, if Dan works in the United Kingdom the first half of the year, and Jessica works in the United Kingdom the second half, this could be enough to qualify as an "ongoing presence."

One way that companies may try to avoid this hassle, or to simplify the process of employing workers in many jurisdictions, is to use a local contracting company referred to as an Employer of Record (EOR).[8] Several all-remote companies have also mitigated this problem by collaborating with a Professional Employer Organization (PEO), which administers payroll and benefits on behalf of the all-remote company.[9] This shifts most of the fiscal and legal responsibility of employment within a given country or territory away from the company and onto the EOR or the PEO. The company is freed from the requirement of setting up a legal entity in the new location, and the EOR or PEO instead uses its local expertise to ensure that any contracts with residents remain in compliance with local taxation and labor laws. This process is especially helpful if a company employs only a limited number of workers in a new location. Over time, if the workforce in that location grows, it may become worthwhile for the company to establish its own local entity with corresponding legal and HR departments.

In my discussions with companies, I have also found that WFA workers are often hired as contract workers but with higher wages (as compared to permanent workers) to compensate for their lack of benefits. There are some countries that have enacted legislation targeted toward remote workers. For example, while workers on a digital nomad visa in Portugal are exempted from paying local income tax, the country has rolled out new taxation rules for anyone engaged in cryptocurrency mining and trading.[10] In Costa Rica, meanwhile, digital nomads are welcome but must provide proof of private health insurance for the duration of their stays.[11] During the process of implementing WFA, I encourage companies to be aware of the regulatory framework in the countries its workers live in, and consider how differences in regulations across these countries could affect the company's workers—and the company.

Digital Nomads and the Spatial Distribution of Future Talent

As more people become able to work from anywhere, the question of where employees *want* to work and live becomes increasingly important. While some workers have clear preferences, for instance wanting to move close to existing friends and family or to more affordable locations, many have other priorities, like wanting to live near a beach, or near restaurants and museums, or just somewhere with temperate weather.

Some, known as digital nomads, even move from one place to another, spending weeks or months in one place before moving on to the next, all while still working full-time, completely remote jobs. For these flexible workers, a whole host of locations become potential places to call home. And in response, locations hoping to attract these remote workers—and their tax dollars and local spending—have begun offering incentives for them to move to their town, region, or even country.

Within the United States, this phenomenon has taken the form of a slew of cities and states creating programs to bring remote workers to their areas. In Northwest Arkansas, the region highlights its outdoor activities and offers a mountain bike for newcomers, along with cash incentives.[12] Topeka, Kansas, offers up to $15,000 in housing assistance for qualified remote workers.[13] And West Virginia offers wraparound services including housing cost reimbursements, access to coworking spaces, and funding for professional development.[14]

The idea of bringing in remote talent with a combination of cash incentives and connecting them to the local community through social programming was pioneered in Tulsa, Oklahoma, by the Tulsa Remote program, which launched in 2018 with a class of one hundred remote workers. The goal was to attract community-minded workers who would become engaged city residents, and hopefully stay long after the one-year program requirement. Program participants ended up volunteering at the local high schools, serving on local boards, and even opening new businesses.[15] By one measure, the Tulsa Remote program generated nearly $14 of increased economic activity for every $1 it spent on incentives for participants.[16] For local governments hoping to boost their economies, this financial benefit is a clear argument in favor of attracting more remote workers.

Globally, since 2019, forty countries and territories have rolled out their own incentive programs aiming to attract digital nomads. Places as diverse as the Seychelles, Portugal, Brazil, the UAE, Costa Rica, and Estonia now offer digital nomad visas that allow for temporary residence.[17] Each country's program is slightly different, but broadly speaking, the visas span from three months to one year and exempt the workers from local taxes in exchange for a one-time fee. Some places, like Portugal, even allow digital nomads to eventually transform these short-stay visas into permanent residence after a certain period of time.[18] All of the programs require that the visa holder provide proof of employment in a remote workplace—allowing governments to sidestep the contentious issue of immigrants taking jobs away from local residents, while still benefiting from the workers' relatively higher incomes and spending habits. See appendix A for more details on different countries' policies for digital nomads.

So, what does the expansion of digital nomad programs mean for you as a manager? If your company is embracing WFA, these programs add yet another level of flexibility for your remote talent. For workers who are interested, help them look into programs that could be right for them. If your company is interested in experimenting with WFA, sponsoring certain workers for fixed-term digital nomad programs is one way for you to offer the benefits of WFA even to your staff that can't permanently move.

One popular option is what's known as the workcation, where workers can combine vacation days with remote work to take extended trips. Google, for instance, now allows its workers to spend four weeks per year working remotely from anywhere, even as it expects most workers to return to the office for the majority of their working time.[19] Another model is that of Cisco, which brings members of its global workforce to Venice for several months at a time through its Venywhere program (Cisco headquarters is in

Venice, and the program is a play on the words *Venice* and *anywhere*).[20] These can be great opportunities for workers to explore new places, or take longer visits home to see family. Companies can also take advantage of infrastructure designed for digital nomads, such as the digital nomad villages set up in places like Startup Madeira in Portugal or Nomad Village Brazil, to gather teams together for an offsite or to create opportunities for workers to travel to locations that are specifically set up to greet these types of work and tourism travelers.

WFA is the future: it's a win-win-win for companies, individuals, and communities alike. This unique work arrangement positions companies to hire diverse talent from anywhere, helps individuals live within their ideal locations, and has the potential to empower smaller cities, towns, and places that experienced brain drain by attracting new talent. WFA triggered the digital nomad era, with countries and regions now competing for remote workers. And the pace of WFA adoption is being accelerated by technology, especially digital twins, which leverage the automation-sensor-AI revolution. These changes will ultimately enable a more equitable future where workers across almost all industries will be able to work from anywhere.

Part Two

Managerial Strategies to Implement WFA

For all the benefits WFA can provide to employers, there has been a vigorous debate about the adoption of this work arrangement. There are still a lot of WFA and remote-work skeptics, and with good reason. In the minds of many leaders, "work" is conflated with "office" (the default performative stage for work) and accepting a new normal will require adopting new beliefs and changing existing behavior. Decades of research indeed establish that some tasks, such as mentoring and building team norms, are better done in person. It's not tipping my hand to say that I think each and every one of these obstacles can be overcome with the right set of management practices, and that the value of WFA greatly outweighs the potential challenges. But to decide whether WFA is right for your company—and importantly, to figure out how to account for trials you might face as you implement a WFA model—it is helpful to first acknowledge and then address these concerns directly, and to understand a set of management practices that mitigate any issues.

Most criticisms of WFA operations boil down to three main problems: communication, knowledge sharing, and isolation. Chapter 3 will shed light on the communication problem and its solutions: dealing with communicating across space and time and ensuring that workers communicate effectively when they cannot do so face to face. Chapter 4 will highlight solutions to the knowledge-sharing problem: how workers can learn everything they need to know to do their jobs effectively without barging into someone's cubicle or tapping on the shoulder of a colleague, and how to be sure that all information remains up to date. Chapter 5 will focus on solutions to the isolation problem: the dual challenge of workers' social and professional isolation in a WFA setting. How can managers ensure that workers are feeling connected to their team and the broader company, and have access to the learning and mentoring opportunities they need to grow and advance in their careers? Finally, chapter 6 summarizes a transition plan, going from a traditional hybrid work arrangement to WFA in stages. In brief, I make the argument that teams should dictate the pace of the transition, allowing for bottom-up experimentation rather than mandating a uniform top-down policy. In this second part of the book, you will come to understand the secret sauce of WFA management practices.

3

WFA and Communication

For managers considering a shift toward WFA, one of the top challenges to be addressed is the intraorganizational communication problem. By distributing employees across the world, WFA forces teams to work across distant work locations and at different times of day, making communication difficult. As Apple's Tim Cook puts it: "My gut says that, for us, it's still very important to be physically in touch with one another, because collaboration isn't always a planned activity . . . innovation isn't always a planned activity. It's bumping into each other over the course of the day and advancing an idea that you just had. And you really need to be together to do that."[1] This sums up a key concern managers have with WFA: How can you bring colleagues together in a way that allows them to communicate effectively? Relatedly, how can you capture the spontaneity of office interactions? People often cite the watercooler effect: a spontaneous interaction in which you run into a colleague from another team, and in your chatting, learn about a potential opportunity that could help everyone. How can a WFA setting facilitate these types of chance meetings, as well as the later positive effects?

There is a range of literature that lends weight to these concerns. Scholars studying effective communication discuss several ways that miscommunication can occur between colleagues. Common problems can include using poorly defined terms, misunderstanding each other's language, context, or tone, or even relating to silences in conversations in different ways. Face-to-face interaction tends to minimize these issues and provides the opportunity for real-time questions and feedback between colleagues.[2] This can be particularly true for information that is difficult to put into writing; instructions for how to fill out a form may be easier to convey over email than the texture a ball of dough should be before it is ready to be shaped into a loaf.[3] Firms implementing WFA policies take the communication problem seriously as well. Even the organizations most committed to WFA and working asynchronously across time zones concede that certain conversations and certain types of information are best conveyed during face-to-face interactions (although generally over a video messaging application like Teams or Zoom rather than in person).[4]

However, it is important to note that the communication problem is not a new one, nor is it unique to WFA workplaces. Multinational corporations have long operated with workers spread across distant time zones and in far-flung locations. The Dutch East India Company had offices at either end of the Eurasian continent in the 1600s. Much has been written on how these firms can more effectively spread company norms, manage distant personnel, and operate across cultural and physical distances.[5] Even in a single firm location, the odds of spontaneously interacting with any single coworker remain small. Apple's Cupertino campus, for instance, spans 360 acres. How likely is it that workers are interacting with someone on the other side of that campus? In another building? On another floor? A classic workplace study from 1977 may have some answers for us. In studying how information moves through the workplace, Thomas J. Allen found that distances as little as ten meters between coworkers reduced the likelihood of spontaneous interaction significantly, and that being farther than twenty-five meters apart reduced it to effectively nothing.[6] In my own case, I am more likely to bump into colleagues working on the fourth floor of the building (where I work) on the Harvard Business School (HBS) campus, rather than serendipitously meeting colleagues working on other floors or in other buildings of the HBS campus. Working in person may lead to more face-to-face interactions, but not necessarily to interactions with new and different colleagues, or people with novel information to share. Whether a firm is located on one sprawling campus or distributed globally, bringing the right people with the right information together to collaborate in an effective and innovative way will remain a challenge.

Solving the Communication Problem

One solution that all-remote and remote-first offices use to address this challenge is asynchronous communication, any interaction that does not require two people to be actively involved in a communication process at the same time. Emails, memos, and text messages or online chat platforms like Slack are asynchronous communication. Even a recorded video message can be asynchronous communication. A video call, telephone call, or in-person conversation, on the other hand, are examples of synchronous communication, where two or more participants are expected to speak and respond in real time.

Companies operating across many locations or time zones often rely on asynchronous communication, both due to the logistical challenges of having team members who work very different hours and due to the benefits of having written records of communications and the production of work. The exact policies each company pursues are likely to be tailored to their own company culture, goals, and team distribution. I will share examples of asynchronous communication practices from two organizations I studied in detail: GitLab and Doist. As these two examples illustrate, companies that adopt largely asynchronous communication practices also tend to organize the production of work as an asynchronous flow.

GitLab, an all-remote software as a service (SaaS) company that employs over one thousand workers worldwide, can serve as an example of what a reliance on asynchronous communications looks like. At GitLab, the primary platform for worker interactions is GitLab itself, which is an asynchronous collaboration tool. On the GitLab platform, each worker is assigned a set of issues or basic tasks, which they complete and pass on to (or get input from) colleagues using what they call a merge request. Once a task is finalized, it is committed into the GitLab master file. This system runs entirely asynchronously, with one worker completing a task and then sending it for feedback from peers, supervisors, and even the public before that task is finalized. The GitLab team is encouraged to complete their work using the GitLab platform, and nearly all of the information on that platform is visible both internally and externally to the public. In interviews, GitLab employees highlighted for me how the asynchronous nature of working on issues helped them seek feedback early on. In other words, once an employee worked on an issue, they could seek and receive feedback on the issue asynchronously and revise their work accordingly. Instead of producing a fully baked product and presenting it at a team meeting, only to realize how much it could be improved, the asynchronous workflow at GitLab enables employees to receive feedback in small drips and improve their work incrementally and continuously. In sum, the thoughtful use of asynchronous communication leads to an asynchronous form of coordinating work. In other words, when division of tasks, communication, and delivering feedback are all done asynchronously, teams engage in asynchronous coordination.

Even when Gitlab does choose to engage in synchronous communication (usually in the form of a videoconference), the company has processes in place to allow the information in that context to be viewed and interacted with asynchronously. Ahead of a video call, the company will circulate a shared agenda document, which allows team members in distant time zones to react to the planned discussion and add questions and comments that can be addressed even if they are unable to attend the call in real time. The calls are then recorded and made available for viewing, and the agendas are updated to reflect any policy decisions made during the meetings. Importantly, this framework for asynchronous engagement in meetings is also coupled with a strict understanding that workers will not participate in meetings that occur outside their established work hours.

Another example of a WFA firm focused on asynchronous communication is Doist, a global app developer with over one hundred employees in thirty-five countries worldwide. Doist also emphasizes an asynchronous-first way of working. And like GitLab, the primary way they do so is by using their own asynchronous communication product—in Doist's case, the Twist communication app. Twist is designed to be a combination of an email server and instant messaging platform, but with elevated searchability and less gamification. The platform also encourages transparency, with team-level and company-level searchable threads on ongoing projects and other topics (though there is also a private, direct message function as well). This has the added value of past threads serving as an institutional knowledge base for anyone wanting to understand why or how a past decision was made (more on this and the importance of documentation for WFA firms in chapter 4).

Doist as a firm pushes for fewer meetings and more independence in scheduling for its workers. Once a project has an initial kickoff meeting, that team may only have biweekly check-ins, with the bulk of communication happening instead in Twist threads. Team members contribute to those Twist conversations regularly and use the conversations to inform their ongoing work, but there is no expectation for immediate responses. Instead, team members are pushed to reflect and consider their ideas before sharing them. As one Doist manager explained, though the process may take longer, the company found that asynchronous discussions lead to better outcomes:

> It feels sacrilegious to say this, especially at a tech company, but at Doist we don't whiteboard. That's because the ideas people bring to the group, presented in writing in threads, tend to be of higher quality than those that are spitballed or shouted out in meetings. Twist also offers a more level playing field, in that the ideas that win out are less likely to belong to individuals with senior positions or with the loudest voices.[7]

As at GitLab, Doist pairs this asynchronous-first communication style with dedication to the idea that work quality is more important than the number of hours spent on a problem. Though some Doist team members opt to work nonlinear schedules (like combining a two-hour midafternoon break with some evening hours, or working around childcare schedules), there is a broad agreement that individuals can decide how long to work based on what they need week to week—and importantly, ideally no one should consistently be working weekends.

Benefits and Challenges of Asynchronous Communication

Two main benefits accrue from adopting asynchronous communication and workflow practices: the generation of more thoughtful ideas by workers and enhanced temporal flexibility for individuals.[8]

Asynchronous communication may result in the generation of higher-quality ideas and may encourage a more diverse set of employees to participate in brainstorming sessions. As HBS professor Teresa Amabile has argued, creativity in the workplace relates to the production of novel and useful ideas.[9] Asynchronous communication may foster workplace creativity by forcing individuals to write down their ideas. In an interesting study, researchers Anne-Laure Fayard (Polytechnic School of Engineering, New York University) and Anca Metiu (ESSEC Business School) look at how writing supports dialogue and collaboration between distant colleagues. The researchers find that writing has three unique benefits: it forces individuals to objectify and contextualize their ideas, focus on specifics, and reflect on their ideas.[10] In fact, there has also been a long-standing academic debate on whether brainstorming (the contemporaneous generation of ideas in face-to-face interactions) or brainwriting (the process of sharing written-down ideas without being watched) leads to the generation of better-quality ideas.[11] Brainwriting has the benefit of individuals not feeling watched while they generate their ideas, and a recent study claims that the quality of ideas was comparable when brainwriting was conducted in person versus online.[12] This might be especially advantageous for introverts, and prior research shows that shy individuals feel less communication apprehension during the discussion conducted online.[13]

Asynchronous communication can also lead to a reduction in the number of meetings that workers are required to attend, enabling them to have a greater voice in when they work. Recent research shows that once companies introduced even one "no-meeting day" per week, employees reported a greater sense of autonomy, engagement, and satisfaction, and lower levels of stress or the feeling of being micromanaged.[14] Management research has long established that employees can experience better work-life balance when they have a greater voice in when they structure their work.[15] In fact, along with geographic flexibility and work from anywhere, employees have been advocating for greater agency on temporal flexibility, the flexibility to decide when to work.[16] Asynchronous communication processes can empower workers with increased control over their work schedules and design a WFA experience that grants them both geographic and temporal flexibility.

However, the use of asynchronous communication technologies also entails two significant challenges: fueling dopamine production and increasing worker distractions, and shrinking the communication networks of workers. A large body of research has explored brain (intracranial) stimulation to reward centers and dopamine release, especially in experiments involving animals and food rewards.[17] There are specific parallels between work done by psychologist B. F. Skinner on rats and how their behavior is shaped by food rewards and the constant feedback modern workers receive from technology applications.[18] Communication apps like Slack and Teams are designed to provide rewards (in this case, likes or comments rather than food) and encourage ongoing engagement. This dynamic can intensify in a work environment, both because workers are *required* to use these apps and because of the way they've been introduced to the workplace. Often, rather than replacing traditional reporting, the apps are added on top of existing workflows. So even if a worker has responded appropriately to a thread or issue, they will still need to send an email to their supervisor, adding redundant work to their load.[19] This additional workload, along with the constant thrum of new inquiries or tasks requiring their attention, can lead workers to feel overwhelmed and have trouble prioritizing tasks or appropriately dividing their time among projects.[20] This task dysfunction can also be disastrous to workers' ability to focus, and research by psychologist Gloria Mark (University of California, Irvine) suggests that for every interruption (whether a knock on an office door or a digital inquiry), it can take more than twenty minutes for a worker to get back to their initial task.[21]

Overdependence on asynchronous communication has also been shown to have negative effects on the size of workers' professional networks. During the Covid-19 pandemic, for example, researchers found that workers' networks shrank by just under 16 percent on average.[22] They attributed this decrease to the tendency of workers—and everyone, really—to reduce contact with their broader networks and acquaintances, and instead focus on their closer relationships, whether direct collaborators or friends and families. In the workplace, this focus also has the effect of intensifying silos. If someone communicates only with their direct collaborators, it makes them much less likely to engage in the casual conversations with colleagues with different roles or expertise—interactions that have previously been shown to be key sources of novel information and drivers of innovation.[23]

Best Practices for Successful Asynchronous Communication

What can a company do to benefit from asynchronous communication practices and asynchronous workflows while mitigating the challenges? Several best practices come to mind. First, leaders need to embrace and demonstrate the power of writing down ideas. This theme will be expanded upon in chapter 4, and I argue that this practice has several spillover benefits. Second, to contain distractions and dopamine hits, organizations can enforce the limits of asynchronous communication. Just as companies have attempted to mitigate Zoom fatigue and meeting fatigue by enforcing "Zoom-free Fridays" or "library rules in the office," boundaries can also be set to limit the extent of asynchronous work.[24] Boundaries might take the form of time blocking practices, wherein individuals block off dedicated chunks of time to devote to heads-down focus, adopting "no-ping" hours, or limiting the amount of information that individuals have to read or react to online.[25] As one Doist employee told me, the idea of asynchronous communication is to surf a lagoon of information that is relevant and useful to the individual, rather than surfing the ocean of information on all company operations. A technological solution that creates the perfect lagoon for each worker and avoids constant pings and dopamine hits relates to limiting the number of colleagues who participate in asynchronous communication channels and restricting the technological settings that result in signals—pings, likes, green light indicators (indicating unread messages), and so forth—that feed dopamine hits. Individuals can also be encouraged to develop and share their preferred style of communication and response times, so that colleagues, especially managers, know what response times to expect.[26]

Ultimately, I believe most WFA workplaces will adopt a mix of synchronous (face-to-face) and asynchronous communication practices—in fact, many already have. One path for managers seeking to encourage more asynchronous communication is to select one of their lower-risk projects as an environment to test this new process. This pilot can also serve as an opportunity to develop team norms around how to use asynchronous communication. For instance, one team I worked with developed a best practice of brainwriting ideas and scheduling a brief call at the end of the week to prioritize them. The team also held the standard that brainstorming ideas *during* the Friday call was prohibited. The logic was simple: Everyone on the team had all week to read, reflect on, and react to the ideas that had been brainwritten. It would be unfair to brainstorm an idea now and not allow colleagues the same time to reflect and react to it. This system—and whatever norms your team chooses to establish—will allow for a functional balance between thoughtful reflection and creative conversation, as it's clear that the future of communication will require both.

4

WFA and Knowledge Sharing

The knowledge-sharing problem is another challenge workplaces hoping to implement WFA policies need to address. Separate from the communication problem discussed in chapter 3, critics worry that a distributed team or workforce will struggle to learn (and remain up to date on) the information needed to complete their tasks. As Microsoft CEO Satya Nadella explained in an interview discussing hybrid work at the company, "[Physical office] space is the ultimate collaboration tool that was refined over a two-hundred-year period … we're not just going to trade it away, [even if now] we're going to use it, perhaps, differently."[1] Nadella addresses the concern managers have with remote work: If in-person collaboration is best for teams, especially teams focused on creative or innovative work, how can remote teams still come together to create, innovate, and problem-solve? And in particular, how can you do this for teams that are *extremely* geographically distant, to the point that a videoconference call might not be an option? Like the communication problem, this issue grows more complex as teams are farther apart in time zones. When each worker may be operating during a time when they are the only team member online, how can you ensure that each person has the information they need to do their job? And as that information changes, how can you be sure that all team members continue to have the most recent and relevant information, so they are able to keep iterating and moving that idea forward? Moreover, how can new hires learn from senior colleagues if they cannot walk into their cubicles or offices and ask them questions in real time? How do workers benefit from vicarious learning (observing and modeling the actions of mentors) and social learning (enabling workers to avoid costly mistakes that others might have already committed and learned from)?[2]

Remote work advocates also concede that the question of accessing the most recent information asynchronously (whether due to flexible scheduling or distant time zones) remains one of the thorniest of the remote workplace. Senior workers at GitLab mentioned several ways that accessing information can pose a problem for them, even in a company dedicated to operating in a remote and asynchronous way. One engineer relayed a story of a work product that was handed off without adequate documentation to a team member in a later time zone. The colleague was left with no idea of where to start or what still needed to be fixed, forcing them to either guess (with the possibility of guessing wrong and working on the incorrect task) or wait until their teammate got online to clarify, which might not be for eight or nine hours.[3] Other GitLab workers noted that to operate this way, they are constantly thinking several steps ahead to accommodate team members operating during different work hours. One web post, for instance, might take an extra day to prepare due to the fact that the writer is in California and the editor is in London. This extended timeline is manageable, of course, but only if both the writer and the editor are conscious of the ways their work timing affects each other.

My own work across time zones highlights the different ways that workers can try to accommodate the need for knowledge sharing with far-flung teammates. Along with my collaborators Jasmina Chauvin (Georgetown) and Tommy Pan Fang (Rice University), I looked at how communication by distant teams changed in response to daylight saving time, which affected time zone difference by an hour or two. We found that increasing the temporal distance between teammates led to a 9 percent decrease in synchronous (video calls like Zoom or text chats like Slack) communication.[4] For teams focused on knowledge-intensive work, however, these teammates were more likely to make up for this loss of immediate communication by setting aside time outside of their normal business hours for synchronous communication. For instance, a team member in Singapore might start work early and take a call at 7 a.m. their time, while their counterpart in New York City might stay late until 7 p.m. local time to make the same call. We found that teams working on routine tasks, in contrast, were more likely to rely on asynchronous communication like email. These patterns show that even teams that *are* finding ways to share information and collaborate in a remote setting can sometimes be solving one problem by creating another, namely upsetting their work-life balance in the interest of working effectively. Our study, however, offers an important caveat: we found that female employees and employees based in countries with stricter legal work hour limits engage in significantly less time-shifted communication.

Solving the Knowledge-Sharing Problem

In the context of WFA, solving the knowledge-sharing problem entails asking the following: How can workers learn everything they need to know to do their job effectively *in real time,* and be sure that information remains up to date? While the communication problem centers on the need for ensuring that team member inputs—work, ideas, notes, messages, and even feelings—are communicated in real time with other team members, the knowledge-sharing problem focuses on the need for *organizational* information, for example, procedural information related to best practices. For example, how do we apply for additional budget here? How do we reduce waste on the shop floor? How do we ensure hiring practices encourage diversity and inclusion? All organizational information (a section of code, the release schedule for a product in development, or how the company wants its recruiting team to advertise a new role) must be available in real time to all relevant workers. One solution that WFA offices use to tackle this challenge is a practice known as knowledge codification.

Knowledge codification is the process of turning tacit but codifiable information into an organized—and importantly, searchable—resource.[5] This means writing down exactly how a company performs its key activities and creating a how-to document that remains online and accessible to all company employees. Many workplaces have some sort of company handbook that new hires receive, but those usually include some broad policies like how time off is accrued, and legal information about employees' rights and workplace safety. Prior research has also outlined several challenges of ensuring successful knowledge codification. Organizational scholars Morten Hansen (University of California, Berkeley) and Martine Haas (University of Pennsylvania) point out that the quality of written documents is regularly poor, and codification is often incomplete.[6] The authors refer to consulting firms and state that written documents frequently convey facts and figures, rather than deep nuanced insights (which are usually shared in person during client presentations). The knowledge provided in these codified documents is also often outdated and contextually irrelevant. In addition, the act of searching for codified knowledge may require a lot of time and effort.

Many companies have solved this problem using the "tap the shoulder" approach, which can look like the following scenario of a new HR assistant: I have just taken a job as an HR assistant at Megacorp. Most of my job involves tracking workers' paid time off and ensuring we have enough coverage to operate every day. My onboarding involves learning how to respond to sick day and vacation time requests and to create weekly schedules. So, my knowledge base is to leave requests and schedule reporting and maybe some spreadsheets tracking employees' remaining days off for the year. Two weeks in, however, someone reports that they need to go on parental leave. I have not learned how the company handles this sort of request, so I tap the shoulder of my colleague or supervisor and ask. They point me to the correct form or response format, and I complete the process. And so on . . .

At a WFA company, however, I (the new HR assistant) do not have a colleague or supervisor physically present to ask about the process for responding to a parental leave request. In fact, my supervisor might be located five or six time zones away, and not be active online to respond to my query at all. So where do I turn for this necessary information? In an effective WFA workplace, I would look to a source of information like an online company handbook, where I could search "how to respond to parental leave request" and find the correct policy and procedural information I need to complete my work task *in real time*.

Benefits and Challenges of Knowledge Codification

For codification to work effectively, a company must create documentation for every policy, process, and potential question they can think of, including entries for everything from "how to file an expense report" and "who grants permission for a media interview," to "how the company determines quarterly sales goals." This can be a great thing, as it takes all the institutional knowledge of a company that would normally be stored in employees' brains or inboxes and moves them to a centrally shared location. However, this can also be a daunting process, which takes a long time to create and results in a lengthy document that will need continuous updating as processes and policies change—forever.

This is a tricky problem to solve, given the incentives and motivation of workers to codify knowledge. Workers often view codification as overhead and not work itself. This is particularly true for workers who enjoy in-person interactions and do not like writing down what they are working on or what they have learned as experts. In fact, as Hansen and Haas have shown, experts who pursue a less-is-more strategy by providing high-quality documents only on a few selected topics gain more attention from knowledge recipients—thereby creating a perverse incentive for experts to codify only knowledge on select, high-profile topics and not mundane topics such as the policy for granting leaves.[7]

Another problem of knowledge codification that has been highlighted in prior research relates to having multiple sources (rather than one single source) of truth within organizations. In an influential 2001 study, Hansen and Haas documented how information might reside within multiple documents (written by several document owners) and how workers searching for information may not consider all the sources of information, instead being more likely to defer to high-profile providers of it.[8] As a result, information accessed by workers may be incomplete or even incorrect.

Best Practices for Successful Knowledge Codification

Solving the knowledge codification problem (ensuring that all relevant information is codified and available as a single source of truth in real time) is a challenge for any organization, but it is a critical requirement for a WFA company, given their inability to use the shoulder-to-tap approach. There are two schools of thought on how a WFA company can tackle codification: the whole-team approach and the special-team approach.

The whole-team approach is one in which all employees are expected to engage in documentation and contribute regularly to the company's knowledge codification process. The special-team approach is one in which a team at a company is tasked solely with the collection, recording, and management of this codifiable and codified information. In practice, most companies do a combination of these two approaches, with everyone expected to contribute to codification, but also creating a team tasked with managing the process and checking the quality of the codification (clearly written, thorough, and accessible to others).

GitLab once again serves as a useful real-world example of how this process can work. To solve the knowledge codification problem, GitLab organically created a handbook repository to answer any question that starts with the word *how*. This is how GitLab leadership describes the handbook: "The GitLab team handbook is the central repository for how we run the company. When printed, it consists of over 2,000 pages of text. To uphold the GitLab value of being transparent, the handbook is open to the world, and we welcome feedback. Please make a merge request to suggest improvements or add clarifications. To ask questions, use issues."[9]

For a GitLab team member, participating in knowledge codification is considered *part* of their daily work, listed alongside their other tasks on their work dashboard. It is expected that, in addition to, say, drafting a section of code, an engineer will also complete documentation about what the code means, why they completed this task, and how far they got toward finishing it. That way, as they finish their workday, another engineer on the team is able to pick up immediately where they left off and continue moving the task forward. In fact, in early 2020, Sid Sijbrandij, the founder and CEO of GitLab, told me that he spends close to an hour each day codifying knowledge, behavior that acts as a great signal for his direct reports to follow suit. An HR manager at another all-remote company told me that during their hiring interview, they tell potential employees, "You will enjoy geographic flexibility and decide where to work, however, for this work arrangement to work out, you will need to write down and codify your work in real time. Writing down what you have worked on and learned is part of your job here."

As for accessing information, GitLab team members are supposed to check with the company handbook for the official way to complete tasks, rather than asking a colleague. If a team member indeed has a question that the handbook does not answer, it becomes their responsibility to reach out to the appropriate team members, find an answer to that question, and ensure that the answer is recorded in the handbook for the next person looking for this information. This focus on codification also affects how GitLab team members communicate and interact with one another. If an employee messages their manager with a question about how to, for instance, file an expense report, that manager is most likely to respond by sending a link to the relevant page of the handbook rather than sending a Word document or PDF attachment with the policy details. This kind of response provides the needed information, while reinforcing the idea that the manager's direct report could have (and should have!) turned to the handbook first, before asking a colleague. The handbook at GitLab is indeed the single source of truth, a unique resource created using the principle of crowdsourcing.

Social science research has a term for the process where a group of individuals, each working independently toward a shared goal, manage to build something complex. This process is called *stigmergy*. The term is most often used in biology, when discussing resources such as ant or bee colonies, but has also been applied to Wikipedia—arguably the most familiar example of collective knowledge codification.[10] One simple example of stigmergy is how ants manage to find food. Individual ants go out and search for food, then lay a pheromone trail when food is found. Other ants from the same colony then follow that pheromone trail, find the same food source (as long as it remains available), and lay another layer of pheromones as they return. Over time, the pathways that lead to food sources are reinforced by the volume of ants using them repeatedly. Pathways that do not lead to food, or that once led to food but no longer do, instead fade over time. In this way, an ant colony can work collectively to create a map to nearby food sources, even if no individual ant has either access to the full map or an intended strategy, beyond finding food with each trip.[11]

In ongoing research with my colleague Thorsten Grohsjean (Bocconi University), we propose that the principle of stigmergy can also be introduced to company-wide knowledge codification by WFA companies.[12] We argue that with each individual writing handbook entries, as well as improving on existing entries whenever they have additional information, the company as a whole is able to create a better overall documentation product than if one contributor or team were to try and replicate this process on their own. This is because each person contributes to the topics that they know best. An argument can be made that the chief operating officer knows the most about company operations. But senior leadership is more likely to know about strategy-level operations rather than about the day-to-day tasks being done by any one contributor or engineer. So, for instructions on how to complete those daily tasks, the company is better served having the engineer—and not the executive—codifying the process. Each entry and each reference to the handbook (such as links to specific pages) then serves as "informational pheromones" that other workers can use when searching for relevant information.

To reiterate, there are two major shortcomings of codification. First, it is a lot of work, and documenting your every action and process is a slog for workers (especially at companies that expect each worker to participate in the codification process). Second, it is a huge amount of information, making it hard for companies to ensure that the information remains up-to-date, high-quality, and easy to search for.

On the issue of incentives and the fact that codification is simply not fun, Darren Murph, a remote-work expert I interviewed puts it simply: "There is a price to pay. The question is whether you want that price to be in documenting every day, or in being forced to live in a specific location."[13] As he explains it, WFA workplaces are not for everyone, and one way WFA companies can weed out the people who will be poorly suited to WFA work is through codification. People who are so dedicated to having the flexibility to live where they choose that engaging in constant codification work is seen as a low price to pay are precisely the workers most likely to thrive in a WFA environment, and therefore they are the workers that WFA firms should be trying to hire. So yes, engaging in codification—of both work done and processes used—is a task that WFA workers will need to complete consistently for a WFA company to work effectively. It may feel like a slog, but it is the price of entry for geographic flexibility.

One tip for effective documentation emerged from my work with an all-remote company, where we instituted a simple rule: no documents (PDF, Word, Excel, PowerPoint or other files) could be shared between employees; instead, employees were required to share links (the URL) to the specific page of the company or team handbook that had the requisite information within. This simple rule created a strong incentive for all employees to contribute to the handbook, as distributing links to the handbook became the *only* way to share information with colleagues. In instituting a culture of sharing links to the handbook, the handbook became the single source of truth for all relevant information at this company.

On the question of managing the sheer volume of information that accumulates when an entire company is constantly documenting its work and processes, here is where the special-team approach to codification can come into play. Specific workers, or more likely an entire team, can be tasked with ensuring that the company handbook, or other source of company knowledge, is actually useful to its employees. This means engaging in quality assurance, reviewing new entries, improving their writing flow, and removing any duplicate information. They can also work to make the codified knowledge easily searchable, and work with employees to learn how to effectively search the documentation for their queries. Finally, they can provide some oversight of participation, checking in with teams whose rate of documentation is slipping, to make sure that the codified knowledge is up to date. In fact, the best performing WFA organizations have made the quality of knowledge codification an explicit performance metric, as important as work-output-related performance metrics.

5

WFA and Isolation

The isolation problem is the third challenge companies hoping to implement WFA policies need to address. The concept of isolation in the context of WFA can be divided into two buckets. First, that remote workers will become *professionally* isolated, building a smaller professional network and having fewer opportunities for learning and career advancement. Second, that remote workers will become *socially* isolated, with less sense of organizational belonging and buy-in to the corporate culture and goals. Relatedly, the isolation problem raises worries that managers will have a harder time supporting their remote direct reports, and in particular, will struggle to identify workers suffering from burnout. Let's examine each of these buckets in turn.

Professional Isolation

Critics of remote work argue that mentorship, especially for new employees or workers in the early phases of their career, is easier in person. They claim that creating a network of personal relationships is key to continued growth and advancement along one's career path, and that these relationships thrive on short, in-person interactions over time. As JPMorgan Chase's Jamie Dimon explains: "You have to look at the flaws of Zoom world. It doesn't work for an apprenticeship program. . . . You're losing opportunities to meet other people. I think there are cumulative negatives."[1] The concern is twofold: first, that WFA operations will lead workers to have fewer interactions with their peers, supervisors, and other colleagues, and second, that the quality of virtual interactions is lower than that of in-person interactions. They worry that without these personal relationships and the face time workers get with direct supervisors and those higher in the organizational structure during in-office work time, employees will lose out on opportunities to learn, grow, and advance in their careers.

Once again, the literature on these topics finds some support for these concerns. In one of the pivotal studies on productivity in work-from-home workplaces, Nicholas Bloom and his colleagues found that despite increases in productivity among WFH employees, those employees were less likely to receive a performance-based promotion than their in-office colleagues during the twenty-one-month period during and after the experiment.[2] Other studies found that remote workers themselves expressed feeling increasingly professionally isolated and less respected in the workplace the more days per week they worked remotely, and that these feelings were tied directly to workers' perceived lack of mentoring, professional development, and learning opportunities.[3]

Even my own work on this topic suggests that a hybrid approach may be the best way to maximize productivity while reducing the likelihood of isolation. Along with colleagues, I ran a field experiment with one of the world's largest NGOs as it returned from Covid-19 shutdowns in the summer of 2020. We randomized the schedules of workers as they returned to the office, hoping to better understand the difference that WFH versus in-office work had on worker performance. What we found is that those with intermediate levels (23 percent to 40 percent or one to two days per week on average) of in-office work on average self-reported greater work-life balance, more job satisfaction, and lower isolation than colleagues who were in the office for either more time or less. We also looked at performance indicators and found that the performance of hybrid workers was similar to their colleagues'.[4]

It would, however, be an oversimplification to conclude that WFA leads to fewer interactions and therefore WFA workers are more professionally isolated and less likely to advance. Other factors are at play here as well. Career advancement differs at each organization and is rarely based on productivity measures alone. Instead, managers use a range of subjective metrics to determine whom to promote. This subjectivity means that managerial biases matter in determining performance ratings, whether in terms of workers' identities, work styles, and socialization styles, as well as the manager's expectations of actually seeing the workers in the workplace (an extreme form of this expectation that forces workers to show up in the office even when sick has been described as presenteeism), or acceptance of remote work by managers.[5]

The literature bears out this bias. In a 2020 study of federal teleworkers, Myungjung Kwon and So Hee Jeon found that the level of managerial buy-in to allowing remote work had tangible effects on remote workers' sense of organizational attachment and satisfaction.[6] My own work at a major investment bank also provides some insights into how managerial biases might affect advancement in a temporary WFA environment. My colleagues Iavor Bojinov, Jacqueline Lane, and I conducted a field experiment on the organization's remote summer interns. We found that interns selected for additional face time (in the form of short "virtual watercooler" interactions) with senior managers were more likely to receive job offers, if, and only if, the interns and the senior managers shared the same ethnic and gender identity.[7] This result points to the ways that unconscious biases among managers translate to the digital space. Overall, it's clear that a loss of professional advancement opportunities is a risk to the WFA model. Rather than opting out of WFA, however, I think organizations worried about these issues need to rethink how they engage in mentorship and advancement across their entire workforce, remote and distributed or not.

Social Isolation

Meanwhile, critics of WFA claim that company culture—the combination of organizational norms, management style, and worker engagement—can only be absorbed in person, leaving remote workers feeling isolated. As Goldman Sachs CEO David Solomon describes it, "The secret sauce to our organization is, we attract thousands of really extraordinary young people who come to GS to learn, to work, to create a network of other extraordinary people, and work very hard to serve our clients. . . . For Goldman Sachs to retain that cultural foundation, we have to bring people together."[8] At its heart, this critique raises three core issues in a remote setting. First, workers will contribute less to the organization, whether in terms of work product or broader social environment (such as participating in activities, including events like going to happy hours). Second, workers will feel less camaraderie with their colleagues, shifting their workplace from feeling like a family or a team to feeling like an obligation or a box to be ticked. Third, workers will be less committed to the company's overall values and ethos, or fail to sense that they are working toward a shared goal or for a shared reason.

These concerns have some merit. In a 2016 internal report, the US Patent and Trademark Office found that its remote workers billed more than three hundred thousand unworked hours.[9] This error prompted the agency to adopt additional monitoring programs for its WFA workers, though my research shows that this Orwellian monitoring had no effect on productivity. There is also a range of literature that finds remote work associated with lower levels of organizational attachment (that is, remote workers are less likely to say they feel connected to their workplace, or have a sense of belonging to a team).[10] When WFA workers feel less camaraderie with their teams, this feeling can also lead to negative work outcomes. A 2007 study found that when team members were more physically distant from one another, they were more likely to blame negative coworker interactions on internal concerns (they don't like me or they are bad at their job) than external issues (they must be too busy or maybe their internet is slow today).[11] Grievances like this, in turn, can lead to resentment among team members, which further feeds into a sense of detachment. For some jobs—especially those where long hours are the norm among new hires, as in corporate law firms, investment banks, and management consulting—the sense of camaraderie among teammates can be an absolutely crucial part of success. Sharing late nights, ordering in dinner, and working together to finish a project are all key parts of these jobs, which are often held by young, highly paid associates. Moving these types of jobs to a remote setting can definitely undermine this sense of shared work. Talking about the experience of Goldman Sachs associates during the pandemic, CEO David Solomon said that they were working the same long hours associates were always expected to work, but acknowledged, "If all you're doing is a lot of work and looking at a . . . screen, a lot of the things that make that experience so fantastic disappear."[12]

This acknowledgment points to what remote work advocates argue is actually the primary company culture challenge of WFA policies: overwork and burnout. Far from being an opportunity for shirking responsibility and underproducing, many WFA managers argue that their teams instead tend to blur the lines of work and home, and bill more hours than they should, leading to burnout. One WFA tech worker explained it this way: "[The company] will take as much as you will give. . . . There is always a lot of work to do [and at home], there's no one to say, 'Hey, it's 5 o'clock, everyone go home.' My computer is right here . . . and it's easy to forget the time."[13] Experiences during the Covid-19 shutdowns were similar, with workers globally reporting longer hours worked during the pandemic.[14] These longer hours were also associated with several negative effects. A study by the American Bar Association found that among US lawyers, the longer hours and general stress of the pandemic led more to rely on alcohol and other substances, and to seek out mental health support. For a sizable minority, these effects were so bad that they considered leaving the profession altogether.[15]

Ultimately, for some of the critics voicing concern that WFA leaves workers disconnected from the company ethos, the hard truth is that *overwork* (*and not remote or distributed work*) might be a big part of the problem. Goldman Sachs itself dealt with this question in 2022, when a group of first-year analysts used the company's own presentation style to argue to their bosses for an across-the-board raise, based on hours worked and other productivity measures. The company agreed, raising entry-level wages to $110,000.[16]

Solving the Isolation Problem

WFA workplaces commonly use two solutions to tackle the challenge of isolation: virtual watercoolers and short-term visits (often referred to as company offsites). Let's review each of these solutions in turn, defining them and discussing their benefits, before turning to common challenges and the best practices for addressing them.

Benefits of Virtual Watercoolers

Virtual watercooler is a term used to describe a structured opportunity for informal interaction. In physical offices, people often view spontaneous interactions at a watercooler, by a coffee machine, or in a shared lunchroom as a key part of their socialization and a way to build their social network within the company.[17] They may have quick chats with other members of their team or people from other teams or departments. They may cover both work and nonwork topics, and in general, these interactions serve the dual purpose of building a sense of camaraderie, while also sharing information about the company, in general, and their work, specifically. In a remote and distributed context, these spontaneous interactions are far less likely to occur, so some companies seek to engineer them, creating a virtual watercooler event.[18] In fact, Stanford professor and distributed work expert Pamela J. Hinds, and associate professor at INSEAD Mark Mortensen have longstanding research on the benefits of spontaneous communication in distributed teams, and virtual watercoolers could be thought of as an example of engineered spontaneous, informal communication within WFA teams.[19]

Virtual watercoolers can take the form of a set videoconference call on a weekly or monthly basis, with people gathering based on job type, or on nonwork interests like gardening, action movies, or pets. They can also take the form of semi-structured meetings or Q&A sessions between junior employees and managers, or even senior company leaders. Virtual watercoolers are *not* Zoom happy hours, where workers can decide whether to participate and where (in my experience) the same group (of usually extroverts) shows up every time. Unlike Zoom happy hours, virtual watercoolers are designed to facilitate random virtual interactions, so workers do not know in advance whom they will meet. One week they might meet the CEO and another week they could meet someone from sales or accounting. Also, unlike Zoom happy hours, attendance for virtual watercoolers is usually mandatory, ensuring that all workers—not only a group of extroverts—participate. Just as in a physical office, these events are designed to give workers the chance to expand their social ties at work, as well as to learn about the company, its business plans, and its ongoing projects.

An example of a virtual watercooler is one that I and my colleagues Iavor Bojinov and Jacqueline Lane helped set up as part of a field experiment at a large investment bank.[20] The bank's leadership was concerned about the ability of new hires and junior employees to receive the mentoring they needed in a remote environment during Covid-related office closures in 2020. Working with firm leadership, we developed a series of virtual watercooler events, randomized attendance among a group of summer interns, and assessed the effects of those mentoring sessions on the attitudes of both the interns and mentors, as well as the likelihood those interns would receive and accept job offers at the firm.

The virtual watercoolers were limited to groups of four or five interns, all meeting with one senior company leader (including VP-level and C-suite-level employees). The sessions were thirty minutes long and involved an icebreaker with the senior participant and quick introductions of the junior hires, followed by a period in which they could ask questions of the senior leader. While the meetings had no mandated agenda, on average, the leaders answered between five and six questions per session—including what they work on, their professional journey at the organization, and their favorite sports team. Sessions were held weekly over the course of four weeks, and the group of participating interns was randomized each week.

We found that partaking in these virtual watercoolers did have a positive effect on both interns' reported satisfaction with the program and their performance levels (as measured by the managerial review). It is important to point out that the performance review was not conducted by the senior managers attending the virtual watercoolers, but by the middle manager overseeing the remote internships. On average, participating in the virtual watercoolers also increased the likelihood of interns receiving a job offer at the conclusion of the program. These results suggest that this type of event does indeed create opportunities for young workers to network and access mentors in a remote environment, in ways that help them advance further in their careers. As one intern told me later, "I had interned in the physical office in New York last year. Interns were on a different floor than senior leaders, and no intern ever pressed the elevator button and landed on the CXO floor for a serendipitous chat with these senior leaders! The virtual watercoolers were a game changer." We also observed important boundary conditions related to these average trends; that is, the positive effects of the virtual watercooler accrued only when the intern and the senior manager sharing the screen also shared demographic characteristics.

Benefits of Company Offsites

Another way that WFA companies—and in particular, all-remote companies, which do not have company offices and whose staff tend to be more far-flung—strive to create opportunities for networking, mentoring, and team building is through in-person events called company offsites. These offsites tend to be annual, biannual, or quarterly meetups at convenient and attractive locations, which all employees are encouraged to attend and with travel costs reimbursed by the company. Companies may also hold more frequent team-level or department-level gatherings, which could similarly fall under the umbrella of an offsite. The conceptual idea behind designing offsites is that time is a "network good." As researchers Cristobal Young and Chaeyoon Lim argue, the value of time depends on the number of social others who have the same schedule of time available.[21] The company offsite is a mechanism to schedule the largest number of relevant coworkers to show up in the same physical space at the same time, in order to facilitate in-person interactions.

The offsite may or may not occur in a company-owned space, and in general, the gathering is used for a combination of socializing and strategizing. Some WFA teams plan offsites to coincide with sales conferences or other such events where all teams are usually present. An offsite is not just team members working together in a fun location; it is team members coming together to get to know one another and build effective working relationships that they can lean on during periods of remote and distributed work. Importantly, the agenda of the offsite is to focus on activities that build social ties within and across teams, with an emphasis on scheduling mentoring sessions, brainstorming, team dinners, team and company rituals, and so forth. In other words, employees are not expected to spend time on individual tasks (such as writing code, conducting research, or drafting reports) while attending the offsite. Also, designing and enacting a consistent set of rituals at every offsite may help build a sense of identification within the team and company, and might help to shape an all-remote culture.

Every company will have its own schedule and specific goals for a company offsite. Generally, it combines some work-focused functions—strategy meetings, discussing company values, developing a new product feature—with team-building functions. One good example of this is done by the all-remote software company Zapier.[22] Zapier holds two full-company retreats each year, for about five days, in rotating locations. Thus far, the company has only traveled to places in North America, but other all-remote companies have gathered in a range of global hot spots like Prague, Singapore, and other locations.

During Zapier's retreats, the team divides its days in half, with part of each day dedicated to company-focused activities and the other to a physical activity. Over the years, these activities have included hiking, food tours, boating, a tour of a movie set, swimming, a visit to an aircraft carrier, and group games, among many others. When the company was smaller, the company-focused activity was a biannual hackathon, where team members would pitch and vote on ideas prior to the event, and then work in cross-functional teams to develop and launch features in just a few days. Prior tasks included adding accessibility features to the Zapier product and developing a detailed how-to guide for Zapier's company processes. As the company has grown, however, these quick deliverable launches have seemed like a less useful goal for the retreats. The company has instead experimented with having "unconference" sessions, during which people can choose to attend from a list of lecture or discussion topics that (again) are proposed and voted on ahead of the retreat.

Another key part of the company retreat is downtime. Zapier prioritizes holding its retreats in locations that give team members a space to relax and spend unscheduled time together. This idea has taken the form of a shared Airbnb house, or a resort with dedicated socialization spaces for games or swimming. It could also be some sort of ranch or other rural getaway spot. Explained Zapier CEO Wade Foster, "We used to think having a large city nearby would be important but then realized we rarely took advantage of the full city amenities. [Instead, now we try to] have some activities very near the retreat location. Beachside houses, resorts near hiking trails, or places with big games rooms (pool, ping pong, etc.) are great because people can entertain themselves in downtime without driving places."[23]

The goal of these offsites is to build team relationships and give workers opportunities to learn about the company and their roles (and paths for growth) within it. But just how successful are they at achieving this goal? Scholarship suggests that short in-person interactions, like those at company offsites, are enough to build relationships that can sustain future collaboration. Research has found that even short interactions—the length of one academic conference or one discussion session—can be enough of an in-person interaction to establish connections that allow distant colleagues to exchange complex information and collaborate effectively long after the trip ends.[24] These short trips and the new connections made during these trips have also been shown to grant access to new funding sources, whether from workers' own companies or through learning about external funding opportunities.[25]

Similarly, academic research on the economic effects of business trips (which, like offsites, mean that team members come together for several days of intensive collaborative work) has shown that travel between two locations is associated with an increased likelihood of patenting innovations with new collaborators, as well as a boost in economic activity at the travel destination.[26] Along with my colleagues Dany Bahar (Brown University), Do Yoon Kim (Boston College), and Wesley W. Koo (Johns Hopkins University), I analyzed data on flight connectivity and global collaborative patenting to see if the presence of direct flights had an effect on innovation outcomes.[27] We found that a 10 percent increase in nonstop flights between two locations led to a 3.4 percent increase in academic citations and 1.4 percent increase in production of collaborative patents between those two locations. Furthermore, we discovered that the positive effects of an uptick in direct flights were stronger between places with greater cultural or temporal difference. This suggests that short face-to-face interactions had the greatest benefit for potential collaborators with larger communication gulfs to overcome. This echoes past research on the benefits of face-to-face interactions for overcoming cultural distance and teaching corporate norms.[28]

But what about company offsites specifically? With my colleagues Charles Ayoubi (HBS), Victoria Sevcenko (INSEAD), and Sujin Jang (INSEAD), I worked with Zapier to find out.[29] We measured the frequency and quality of employee written communications (specifically focusing on Slack, due to its more informal nature) before and after one company retreat. We then looked at how those communications shifted, based on unplanned interactions at the retreat. We created a proxy for unplanned spontaneous meetings by seeing which team members carpooled to and from the airport—something determined by flight arrival times, and not by any characteristics of the worker (age, gender, or department). We found that attending the retreat and having short unplanned interactions led to more frequent Slack exchanges after the event. We further found that the largest increases in communication occurred between people of the same ethnicity, *unless* they shared the same ride to the airport, in which case individuals connected with folks who were not like them. We argue that this result shows short interactions at company offsites can be effective at building relationships between team members in similar jobs, but they are less effective at building relationships across ethnic silos, unless workers are made to interact in small groups for a short duration of time. In fact, the carpooling might be emblematic of constrained colocation, or colocation in shared physical spaces where individuals might feel comfortable interacting with strangers.[30] Examples of other opportunities for constrained colocation might be in the long registration queues at conferences, and lunch or dinner queues while attending a conference or offsite.

In addition to short daylong or weeklong offsites, some companies may also find that they benefit from longer periods of intense colocation, following the model of startup accelerators like Y Combinator or Start-Up Chile. These programs operate on the model of bringing startup founders and early teams together in one place, to live in the same location for a few weeks or a few months, work intensively on their products, and receive mentorship and potential access to funding. This intensive temporary colocation can help entrepreneurs connect with distant talent and be a formative experience for a new company.

My research with Start-Up Chile illustrates this fact.[31] The program was founded in August 2010, as a reaction to rebuilding the economy of Chile in the aftermath of the devastating earthquake earlier that year. At that time, Nicolás Shea, a founder of the program, was working in Silicon Valley after graduating from Stanford University in 2009. As Shea revealed in our interview, he gathered the second-year Stanford MBAs into the campus cafeteria and asked, "Would you come to Chile?" They declined, so he followed up with "How can I get you to come to Chile?" Then he started to draft the entrepreneurs' wish lists in order to spend a few months in Chile. It boiled down to the following: equity-free money ($40,000 would be enough to live on and work in Chile for six months); a working visa (that could be easily renewed); and support with the local bureaucracy associated with living and launching a business in Chile. Shea told me:

> We wouldn't have to convince entrepreneurs to stay in Chile forever, but just for six months—maybe as a stopover on their way back home, as many were immigrants in the U.S. Most of them were about 25 years old. In Chile, they would receive free government money and could forget about lawyers or pitching to investors. Also, Chile is a beautiful country, and it even shares some geographical similarities with California. A friend says it's California squeezed and upside down, where you can go snow-skiing and surfing on the same day.[32]

My research revealed that since inception, the program supported around 2,550 startups and more than 5,000 entrepreneurs from eighty-nine countries. Approximately 25–30 percent of participants were Chileans and the rest, foreigners (largely Americans, Argentines, Indians, and Brazilians). Many of the entrepreneurs had hired local Chilean talent and maintained connections with Chilean entrepreneurs long after they left the country. Some entrepreneurs even met their partners while living in Chile.

One example of the effects on innovation of having talent in one location for an extended period of time is the experience of Doist, a global software company that emerged from the early years of the Start-Up Chile program. Doist's founder, Amir Salihefendic, began hiring locally during his time in Chile, and those hires included a combination of Chilean developers, foreign workers in Chile for the Start-Up Chile program, and eventually expanded to include talent from around the globe. During the early years in Chile, and as a result of the Chilean incubation, Doist developed two applications—Twist and Todoist—that became the basis for their entire business model. The company also developed its corporate culture, investing in creating a remote and asynchronous model that allowed leadership to hire globally while still operating efficiently. These products and models allowed Doist to grow from around 23,000 active users in 2014 to around 1.6 million active users in 2024—and all this developed out of an intense, six-month period of colocation for the founder and his core team.[33]

Challenges of Virtual Watercoolers and Offsites

Something that can limit the efficacy of both virtual watercoolers and offsites is *who* is being brought together and *what* they spend their time doing. Research on collaboration at a distance shows that the most effective teams are ones that have different areas of expertise while also sharing some characteristics, whether in terms of identity or institutional affiliation.[34] So to maximize the benefit of collaboration during short trips, companies should be sure to bring together team members with different specializations or functions within the company. At the same time, however, companies must be wary of relying too heavily on demographic similarities when building personnel networks.

As stated above, experiments on virtual socialization and short bursts of interactions during company offsites have repeatedly found the same pattern of concern: People are more likely to experience successful network building and mentoring opportunities with others who are demographically similar to themselves. In sociology, the tendency of similar individuals to flock together is described as *homophily*.[35] In the case of the Zapier offsite, individuals were exercising homophily based on an observable characteristic, like ethnicity.

There are other limitations of the solutions discussed in this chapter. Our experiment on virtual watercoolers also revealed important differences in how effective the intervention was across racial groups. One such group that did not benefit from the interaction were Asians, and it is possible that the reason is that they were disillusioned to observe fewer Asian leaders at the virtual watercoolers. Our research also reveals the cost of implementing these virtual watercoolers. While all company leaders attending virtual watercoolers face an opportunity cost related to their time and attendance, leaders from minority racial and gender groups face a disproportionate ask in terms of their time and should therefore be compensated for attending a greater share of interactions. The study of company offsites, meanwhile, revealed that, left to their own devices, individuals tend to socialize with those similar to themselves when they are in a physical in-person environment. This pattern is likely to persist irrespective of whether individuals are in the office or attending an offsite, and designers of both in-office days and offsites need to be cognizant of this possibility.

In summary, homophily and shared identity is a common starting place for many work relationships, and if we lived in an equitable business environment with a fair share of racial and gender distribution across the organizational hierarchy, this might not be cause for concern. Unfortunately, the real world is not equitable, and given the identity of most senior executives (white males in the case of Western companies), this finding is troubling. Nevertheless, homophily and bias in the workplace are nothing new, and it is fair to ask whether the biases demonstrated in these experiments on virtual watercoolers and offsite interactions are inherent in the remote and distributed work environment, or merely reflect a troubling truth about our working environment at large. The finding remains important, though, both because identifying a problem is the first step toward remedying it, and because the accessibility and diversity of remote roles is often a key talking point for pro-remote advocates. That real world biases can bleed into remote and distributed workspaces should be no surprise to anyone, but these findings are important reminders that unconscious bias will continue to affect the workplace, even as it moves into the digital realm.

Best Practices for Successful Socialization and Tackling Burnout

So how can remote companies combat bias? I see two paths forward. First is to call attention to the pattern or bias and reiterate the need for diversity, equity, and inclusion trainings in the workplace, as well as to push for inclusive and transparent ways to organize virtual watercoolers and company offsites. As an example, companies organizing offsites may design ample opportunities for individuals to interact in liminal spaces (spaces that allow for spontaneous and yet constrained colocation between diverse individuals, such as carpooling), as discussed earlier. These liminal spaces could be deliberately created in the design of the offsite and should lead to the interaction of individuals across demographic and other silos. A second key way to combat bias is to encourage executives with diverse profiles to spend more of their time engaged in mentoring and networking with younger workers. Crucially, this push should also be accompanied by additional compensation or other incentives for those executives, especially those from groups less represented in leadership, to account for the additional time and effort they would be expected to exert to help companies adjust this imbalance.

Meanwhile, fans of WFA look at the challenges of WFA differently than do its critics. Rather than focusing on communication or isolation as the top concern, WFA supporters repeatedly cite another challenge as their biggest worry: employee burnout. This concern flies in the face of critics' claims that remote workers will be more disconnected or more likely to shirk their responsibilities. Instead, the managers most familiar with WFA—the executives of all-remote companies—say that hyper-productivity and overcommitment is the challenge they deal with most frequently.

For WFA companies, the short-term productivity gains that overwork can drive are not worth the longer-term loss of productivity if and when those workers burn out. Instead, companies with WFA policies tend to take wider views, with two specific solutions to this problem.

First, productivity should be measured based on the quality of work output and not any input to work, including how long individuals work. This is a simple idea but one that is complex to implement, and it requires each task and each job to have a set of measurable metrics against which to judge work quality. For instance, the productivity of a technical writer could be judged based on the quality of writing as measured by the readers of a given report (and not just the manager assigning a score), and the productivity of an IT help desk worker could be measured using the ratio of resolved versus unresolved IT tickets.

Second, each WFA workplace should employ a fully staffed and trained wellness team that proactively looks out for cases of potential worker burnout and assists at-risk individuals with creating a wellness plan. One of the all-remote companies I studied collects worker telepresence data, not for the purposes of measuring productivity, but for the sake of wellness. The data is not shared with managers, only with the wellness team. The wellness team, in turn, works with individuals who stay up late every night of the week or over the weekends, and creates individual plans tailored to fostering work-life balance. Much like with other corporate culture issues, the way this balance can be enforced is through top-down signaling. Company executives must lead by example, finding a way to balance hard work and downtime. This means no sending (or answering) emails at 11 p.m., and actually taking vacation time regularly.

A colleague once pointed out that the biggest critics of remote work and WFA tend to be CEOs leading companies with an ethos of overwork and burnout. For blue-chip investment banks, technology companies, and consulting firms, expecting large numbers of young associates or engineers to work eighty-plus-hour weeks (and then having significant turnover among those young workers) is the norm. Stories abound of CEOs sleeping on the shop floor or scheduling meetings to "meet family." In other words, constant presence, being "seen" by the manager or client, and overwork has been mistakenly considered to be a solution to the social and professional isolation problem—when in fact, they are merely replacing one challenge with another.

6

Transitioning from Traditional Hybrid and WFH Models to WFA

I have outlined why I believe WFA is the future of work, and I have provided pointers to mitigate the communication, knowledge-sharing, and isolation problems in a WFA world. However, if your company is like most, it might still be stuck in a traditional WFH hybrid arrangement. Today, traditional hybrid remains the most widespread work arrangement (see table 1-1), with a series of surveys reporting that American workers consistently favor working remotely at least half of the week.[1] How can your organization transition from a traditional hybrid world to being a WFA company that stays ahead in the talent game?

Transitioning from Traditional Hybrid toward WFA in Stages

Hybrid work is a careful balance of remote days (when the employee can work elsewhere) and in-person days (when the employee travels to a designated company location to work in person). This mix theoretically entails the best of both worlds, offering workers the benefits of flexibility while mitigating the challenges of isolation.

However, it is crucial to note that not all hybrid work arrangements are equal, and there are degrees of flexibility built into the various models, with only some of the most flexible ones effectively positioned for a transition to full WFA policy.

Hybrid work models vary in two key dimensions: the *frequency* of in-person days and the *venue* of in-person days. The variation comes from how often workers need to be in person and where the workers are meeting in person. Some examples of companies engaging in each of these hybrid arrangements are organized in table 6-1. There are three forms of hybrid work, each offering workers varying degrees of flexibility to WFA.

Transitioning from an organization practicing traditional hybrid work to a WFA organization involves two main changes: First is reducing the frequency of in-person days (moving from weekly in-person days to monthly, or even quarterly in-person retreats). Second is flexibility about where teams meet, allowing them to congregate at nonoffice locations such as offsites, conferences, or client locations. Being flexible about the location of in-person days might entail rotating the location of meetups between coasts or countries.

TABLE 6-1

Examples of different hybrid arrangements

	Frequency of in-person days		
Venue of in-person days	**Weekly hybrid (traditional hybrid model)**	**Monthly hybrid (moving toward WFA)**	**Quarterly hybrid (WFA)**
Company offices	Most workers live within commuting distance of company offices (Google, Microsoft, Zoom)	Smuckers	Atlassian, Dropbox, Nvidia/Reddit
Offsite locations	N/A	Functional team offsites at all-remote companies (Zapier, GitLab, Airbnb, Glassdoor)	All-company offsites at all-remote companies (Zapier, GitLab, Airbnb, Glassdoor)
WFA possible?	No	WFA within limited geographic bounds	Yes

Starting from the Traditional Hybrid Model

The first hybrid approach is the traditional one in which workers come into the physical office two or three days per week, every week (referred to as the "weekly" approach for simplicity). This approach is relatively common; survey data from June 2022 found that in these jobs workers spend, on average, 50 percent of their time in the office, or 2.5 days per week.[2] As discussed in chapter 1, adopting this version of hybrid work was a knee-jerk reaction coming out of the Covid-19 pandemic. Given that weekly hybrid work requires employees to be in-person two or three days every week, this is the closest model to being in-person all five days a week, and also the dominant work arrangement of the pandemic era.

After the pandemic, managers were often forced to concede this flexibility. Workers accepted the arrangement as a glass half-full. Needless to say, the traditional hybrid approach does not allow for WFA; instead, the frequency of in-person days is weekly and the venue for in-person days is the company office. Although workers do have some flexibility and save on commute times during their given WFH days, they have a limited ability to work from anywhere or to move beyond comfortable commuting distances from the physical office. The organization also misses out on two of the key benefits of WFA: hiring from a global pool of talent and reducing real estate costs. With workers coming into the office regularly, hiring from afar and downsizing the office in any meaningful way are impossible.

Although more challenging, it is still possible for companies to find ways to implement this approach while accessing a larger talent pool. Zoom, for instance, asked its team to begin working in-person two days per week, but carved out an important exemption to the new policy: workers who lived more than fifty miles from a Zoom office location were not required to meet this requirement, nor were they required to move closer.[3]

To remedy the issue of reducing office rental costs, some companies opt to sublease their spaces or to combine them. Meta, for example, sublet large amounts of its office space in both San Francisco and Austin (although its reduced office needs are probably due to a combination of remote work and corporate layoffs).[4]

If this is the approach your company is currently taking, then I recommend that you allow teams the flexibility to come into the office on a less frequent basis (monthly) and give them freedom to meet in various offsite locations, outside of the office. This is the next step in moving toward a WFA model.

Monthly Hybrid: The Next Step toward a WFA Model

The next step—the monthly hybrid approach—reduces the frequency of in-person work, asking workers to be in the physical office several days per month with every in-person day scheduled during the same week (to minimize travel). The exact week is predetermined by the broader team.

For example, someone who lives in Burlington, Vermont, might drive to their company's office location in Boston and stay there for a week in order to meet their four-or-five-days-a-month requirement. This approach could also be organized as a series of monthly functional offsites, meetings that are organized by functional teams (sales, marketing, HR) to coincide with major events (like a client conference or product launch) that all team members would attend in any case. This kind of work arrangement would also satisfy the condition of having 25 percent of workdays spent in-person.

The monthly approach provides workers with greater flexibility to work from anywhere by expanding their possible living locations to at least the local region (although some people might even choose to fly in, depending on their role and pay scale). It therefore also expands the geography of the talent pool the company can consider when hiring. With fewer people in the office during any given week, companies using this hybrid approach could downsize their office spaces and reduce real estate costs, whether by scheduling teams to be in-person during different weeks of the month, office sharing, hoteling (where workers sign up for available office space on the days they will be in the office), or simply transforming the office into a plug-and-play setup. This approach may also likely see some productivity benefits, relative to either in-office or the weekly approach, as it grants more of the flexibility that drives productivity enhancements in a WFA environment. However, this model also places greater importance on adopting the management practices discussed in earlier chapters that mitigate the isolation challenge of WFA, given that colleagues meet in-person only once every four weeks.

The productivity effects of adopting the monthly hybrid model (vis-à-vis the weekly hybrid model) will probably vary for each company based on the implementation of policies that support WFA and alleviate its challenges. A shift to the monthly hybrid work arrangement should go hand in hand with a company-wide embrace of management policies and supporting processes covered in chapters 3, 4, and 5. In other cases, however, if a company does not change its policies, it may reduce those benefits significantly. For instance, if the company does not think strategically about knowledge codification, virtual watercoolers, and asynchronous communication, then work outcomes could suffer in the three weeks of the month when employees are working remotely. Relatedly, if a company is not thoughtful about arranging the set of tasks being performed while in-person (for example, having people in-office while taking client calls, rather than focusing that in-person time on team building and collaborative work), it too could reduce the potential benefits of this approach.

The next stepping stone to WFA is what I call the quarterly hybrid approach, which gives teams the flexibility to schedule their in-person time on a quarterly basis and allows them to meet at locations outside of the office. This is the ideal WFA setup.

Quarterly Hybrid: The Final Step toward WFA

The third hybrid approach grants workers even more geographic flexibility, by having them gather in person on a quarterly basis or even less frequently (referred to as the quarterly approach). These visits may last longer, perhaps several days to a week, and could occur either at a company office or at another location (many all-remote companies refer to these as an offsite). The in-person days could be timed to coincide with key events on the business calendar, whether to launch a new project or in line with budget approval cycles. It could also involve teams gathering during times when they would have significant in-person requirements anyway—for instance, the week ahead of a fundraiser, hiring activities, or a trade conference. For relatively smaller companies, the quarterly hybrid model could be organized as a set of quarterly all-company retreats.

This hybrid work arrangement echoes the benefits and challenges of WFA. This style of hybridity allows companies to reap the WFA benefit of nationwide, or even global, hiring. Zapier reported 281 employees as of 2019, spread across 17 countries and 163 locations. If Zapier operated like a traditional Silicon Valley startup, it would have been required to hire all 281 employees locally and would be competing against technology giants in hiring such talent.

This model also allows the company to eliminate or significantly downsize its physical office footprint. In fact, companies might also choose to transform the type of physical footprint they have, opting to own a retreat space, for instance, rather than a traditional office building.

On the question of productivity, this style of hybridity grants full flexibility to its workers. However, the long stretches of remote and distributed work in this approach might leave workers vulnerable to feelings of isolation and organizational detachment. To be successful at this quarterly approach, companies need to implement all the relevant processes discussed in chapters 3, 4, and 5 (asynchronous communication, strict dedication to documentation, and virtual as well as in-person mentoring and socialization opportunities), while being thoughtful about how to spend their limited in-person time. As highlighted in chapter 5, short in-person interactions can be enough to combat isolation, develop organizational attachment, and generally build professional relationships that endure throughout longer periods of interacting at a distance. If done strategically, firms can ensure that their quarterly get-togethers accomplish just that, while adding a boost of goodwill and team energy that powers effective communication and collaboration for the rest of their working time.

Allow Teams to Decide the Pace of Transition

This journey from a traditional hybrid to a WFA world should not be a one-size-fits-all, top-down answer. Companies must allow teams to choose for themselves. In other words, the unit of analysis should not be the company or the individual: it should be the team.

This transformation should evolve as a mix of top-down policies and bottom-up experimentation. While leadership may outline broad policies mandating a fraction of workdays that need to be in-person, different teams should be empowered to choose which hybrid work arrangements and what frequency of colocation (weekly, monthly, or quarterly) works best for them.

As an example, company leadership might mandate that all teams need to be in-person for 25 percent of their workdays, and individual teams can choose to structure their in-person time as one day every week (weekly hybrid), one week every month (monthly hybrid), or a longer stretch of time every quarter (quarterly hybrid). It is important that the team considers two sets of factors in making this decision: individual preferences for geography and travel, and how committed the team is to develop and implement the management practices needed to support the chosen hybrid work arrangement.

Teams hoping to implement WFA might plan the transformation to be a stepped transition from the traditional weekly hybrid approach to monthly hybrid, followed by quarterly hybrid. It is clear that I view quarterly hybrid (which allows for unfettered WFA) as the end state that every business leader should aspire to.

Before embarking on this journey with your team, consider the following analytical framework in deciding which step of the progression you should be in at this present moment. Ask two questions: What are the likely productivity effects of WFA for your company, and how much will it cost to move workers to your current firm location?

The answers to these questions will lead you to one of four available answers, as illustrated in figure 6-1. For teams that predict that their workers will see no reductions in productivity, or who might notice a productivity boost, and for whom the cost of relocating their workers between geographies is high, then the best policy would be transition to a WFA model with a quarterly arrangement.

Teams that expect a significant reduction in worker productivity along with a low cost of relocating them should instead operate under the weekly hybrid model. For those falling in the middle, a monthly hybrid approach may be best.

While every team should have the opportunity to create the transition plan that works for them now, there is a clear end state

FIGURE 6-1

Analytical framework to determine the WFA model appropriate for your team or organization

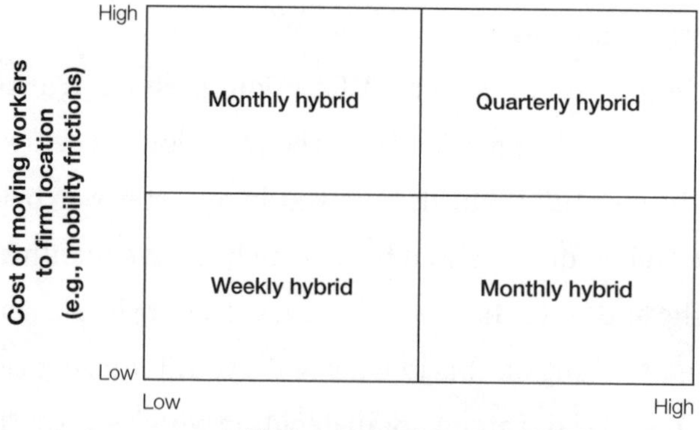

Key factors to consider:

- Quality of management practices to support WFA
- Characteristics of task (e.g., independent vs. interdependent)
- Characteristics of worker (e.g., experienced vs. newcomer)

Source: Adapted from Prithwiraj Choudhury, "Managing the Geography of Work," module note 623-061 (Boston: Harvard Business School, 2023): 16.

that teams should be aiming for. In my opinion, the most effective hybrid approach is one that gives workers the flexibility to work remotely most of the time, with annual or quarterly in-person interactions in the form of company retreats or offsites—that is, the quarterly hybrid model. This is the model that allows for greatest flexibility to WFA and so should be the desired end state. But that end state also needs preparation and significant investment in management practices as outlined earlier. It also requires leadership to make decisions on a few additional questions, especially on the venue of in-person time.

Embrace Management Practices to Support WFA in Phases

Companies and teams planning a transition from traditional hybrid to WFA need to know which management practices to focus on during each phase of the transition. As discussed in chapters 3, 4, and 5, management practices are the secret sauce to make WFA effective. Teams dipping their toe into the future (using the traditional or weekly hybrid approach with workers in the office more than once per week) would be best served to begin implementing policies that are foundational for any and all hybrid work models: scheduling alignment, asynchronous communications, and knowledge codification. In the weekly hybrid model, it is important to ensure that colleagues work in-person on the same days. If half of the team works in-person on Mondays and Tuesdays, and the other half works in-person on Wednesdays and Thursdays, then it may lead to suboptimal social interactions and communication across the team.

Weekly Hybrid Best Practices

Teams following the weekly hybrid model should agree on which days of the week they would spend in-person, with worker surveys suggesting a preference to work from home on Fridays and either Mondays or Thursdays.[5] Ensuring that team members are in-person on the same days is key for positioning them to reap the benefits of in-person work. Otherwise, the weekly hybrid approach could leave you with the worst of both worlds: losing out on global and national hiring, as well as possible productivity gains and cost-savings benefits of WFA, while still facing social and professional isolation.

For the days that employees work remotely, properly codified information allows seamless access to information, and therefore a focus on knowledge codification should be a best practice at all companies. Similarly, asynchronous communication has benefits for the weekly hybrid model by allowing meetings to be clustered during the in-person days and allowing teams to be mostly off video calls on the days they work remotely. Employing these three key management practices will allow companies and teams to move deeper into the realm of hybrid work and explore monthly or quarterly hybrid approaches (if they choose to) down the line.

Monthly Hybrid Best Practices

For teams implementing the monthly hybrid approach, ensuring scheduling alignment between key individuals on a team is even more important. In fact, that scheduling alignment should be your top priority, because if workers are in-person only four or five days per month, it's important to ensure that the entire team shows up for those days to make the most of them and reach the creative thinking, learning and mentoring, and team-building goals that are best achieved during in-person interactions. Companies using the monthly hybrid approach should also prioritize solidifying their knowledge codification and asynchronous communications processes and should also experiment with virtual watercoolers in this phase. With workers remote and distributed for three weeks every month, good communication and knowledge-sharing policies are critical to teams working effectively under this form of hybrid. As your team moves further into the realm of WFA, you should begin to rethink how your company assesses productivity within its teams. Measuring productivity based on quality of output, rather than hours spent (or how many meetings you attended), and ensuring that workers balance work output with personal wellness, will help your company navigate the dual challenges of flexibility and burnout when working remotely.

Quarterly Hybrid Best Practices

Finally, teams embracing WFA and implementing the quarterly hybrid approach should focus on the processes that help them bridge the distance between their workers, notably designing and implementing offsites and virtual watercoolers. Bringing their team members together, whether physically during offsites or virtually through the structured virtual watercooler events, is key to building the team bonds and intracompany networks needed to operate remotely for the remainder of the year. It is important that such companies and teams also design and practice a set of consistent rituals at both the offsites and during the virtual watercoolers, creating a sense of shared identity and belonging in the team and the company over time. These companies should also continue to focus on knowledge codification, which will be leaned on more heavily as company staff grows more geographically distant from one another.

Mastering the Processes for Each Work Arrangement

Because teams are likely to progress in a step-by-step fashion from weekly hybrid to monthly hybrid and then quarterly hybrid, it is important to master the processes supporting WFA in a step-by-step fashion as well (table 6-2). During the phase of weekly hybrid, teams should ace the processes related to schedule alignment (like aligning in-person time for all team members), asynchronous communication, and knowledge codification. In moving to the phase of monthly hybrid, teams should then perfect the processes related to measuring productivity and wellness. Finally, in moving on to the third and final phase of quarterly hybrid, teams should excel in the processes related to planning and implementing offsites and virtual watercoolers, given that the isolation problem is likely to get more acute as teams transition from monthly to quarterly hybrid.

Subsequent decisions need to be addressed, as well, regarding where to schedule the in-person time, and how to spend employees' time together. One creative solution used by some companies in Japan is to meet at centrally located rail stations. A local

TABLE 6-2

Management processes needed for progression from weekly hybrid to quarterly hybrid

	New processes to master		
Management processes	**Weekly hybrid** →	**Monthly hybrid** →	**Quarterly hybrid**
Asynchronous communication	X		
Knowledge codification	X		
Virtual watercoolers			X
Offsites			X
Measuring productivity and wellness		X	
Scheduling alignment	X		

company even decided to install one- and two-person meeting booths in these stations that workers can rent by the hour to hold these meetings.[6] For workers on the go to clients or vendors, these meeting points can serve as a great alternative to a noisy café or traveling to a distant office. Emerging startups like Codi and Radious (both led by female entrepreneurs) are hoping to create a new business model around this concept, by helping teams find appropriate office leases in unique locations, or by helping pair companies to share one lease. Describing themselves as "the Airbnb of commercial rental space," Codi acts as an intermediary between traditional office spaces and companies uninterested in a traditional ten-year lease.[7] Radious, meanwhile, helps workers find space outside of city centers in hopes of helping workers avoid long commutes while also having a place for collaborative work.[8]

These companies might not represent the strategy that works for your company, but each is a great example of how your company can account for your specific needs when tailoring your hybrid approach.

Embrace the WFA Mindset at the Top

Whether your company can successfully implement and benefit from WFA will depend on whether your top leadership and investors are aligned with remote or distributed work and WFA. Shifting the mindset of the leadership team, from executive officers through board members, is the key to success. Commitment to organizational change is most effective when it occurs at every level of management, and companies—and crucially, business leaders—who see this and begin to shift their policies from a traditional hybrid model toward a monthly or quarterly hybrid model will be the ones best able to grapple with changing geography of work, and the unique opportunity to expand talent acquisition through hire-from-anywhere.[9] In sum, a C-suite that both preaches and practices WFA can act as an exemplar and commitment device that ushers in a WFA organization.

Epilogue

WFA and the Future of the Workplace

The global experiment with work arrangements in the face of the Covid-19 pandemic demonstrated that many more jobs can be done remotely and in a distributed fashion than previously assumed. With the expansion of digital twin technologies and advancement of telecommunications tools, it is clear that it will become possible for more and more jobs to be done remotely and in a distributed fashion in the years to come. And based on surveys and conversations with workers across industries, it is apparent that most workers would work remotely if they could.[1] Remote and distributed work—and specifically its most flexible version, WFA—is in effect a strategy to attract and retain global talent, and it is time for company leadership to get on board.

WFA is a win for workers, a win for companies, and a win for society. Workers appreciate the flexibility and quality of life that WFA affords them. Companies are able to access and retain diverse global talent in faraway places and often report higher productivity in WFA environments. Society benefits when people are able to choose to live in places where they may become deeply involved in their local communities, while reducing the negative environmental effects of ever-longer commutes. WFA can act as a counterbalance to the problem of brain drain that has ravaged several smaller towns, countries, and communities. Though the process is challenging, companies can embrace a suite of management practices such as company offsites, virtual watercoolers, knowledge codification, and asynchronous communication, to counteract WFA's downsides and foster effective global workplaces. In addition, WFA companies should build capabilities in working with third-party intermediaries to hire distant talent and administer payroll and benefits (see chapter 2), focus on measuring productivity on output metrics, and measure and ensure the wellness of its distributed workforce. The tools and processes exist; it is now a question of whether company leaders, investors, and managers will decide to use them. Certainly, WFA requires major shifts in management practices, from the ways that teams learn and communicate to the ways companies measure productivity. And the most important factor in whether and how well these shifts take hold at your company is getting the C-suite and the senior management team to buy in to this new way of working.

To close, let me leave you with the things I am sure of. I am sure that WFA works for a wide range of workers, tasks, and industries. I am now convinced that companies and teams can transition progressively from traditional hybrid to WFA, mastering new processes in each step of the journey. I am convinced that the early adopters in a wide range of industries who are experimenting with WFA will gain a competitive advantage in hiring and retaining diverse talent in the decades ahead. I am certain that WFA can unlock talent in new and unexpected places, and that a new class of diverse workers will bring their energy and ideas into sectors across the economy. And I am confident that this transition will require time, concerted effort, and no little bit of faith as managers, investors, and board members are asked to rethink and reprioritize their long-held values. So if you are less sure, know that this journey need not be completed all at once. Every step toward WFA is a step in the right direction. Letting teams experiment with the best practices outlined in this book will serve you well, regardless of how far you venture into the world of remote and distributed work. And if you take the plunge earlier than your competitors, you just may have a leg up in attracting and retaining diverse talent in the future.

Appendix A

Digital Nomad Visa Policies across Countries

The following table summarizes aspects of digital nomad visa policies across countries, highlighting duration, fee requirements, tax exemptions and income requirements.

TABLE A-1

Digital nomad visas by country (as of October 12, 2023)

Country	Maximum stay (months)	Individual visa fee (USD)*	Tax exemptions?	Income requirements? (USD)*
Anguilla	12	$2,000	Income; sales	Proof of employment or business incorporation
Antigua & Barbuda	24	$1,500	Income; sales; import	$50,000 annual
Argentina	12	$200	Income; sales; import	Proof of employment
Aruba	3	$0	Income	Proof of funds to cover stay

(*continued*)

TABLE A-1 (*continued*)

Digital nomad visas by country (as of October 12, 2023)

Country	Maximum stay (months)	Individual visa fee (USD)*	Tax exemptions?	Income requirements? (USD)*
Barbados	24	$2,000	Income	$50,000 annual
Belize	12	$500	None	$75,000 annual
Bermuda	12	$263	Income; sales; import (limited exemption)	Proof of employment or business incorporation
Brazil	24	$127	Income (limited exemption)	$1,500 monthly or $18,000 in bank
Cabo Verde	12	$21	Income; sales; import	Six months of bank statements with at least $1,582
Cayman Islands	24	$1,469	Income; sales	$100,000 annual
Colombia	12	$177	Income (limited exemption)	$2,100 monthly
Costa Rica	24+	$2,219	Income (limited exemption)	$2,500 monthly or $60,000 in bank
Croatia	12	$65	Income	$2,425 monthly
Curacao	12	$299	Income (limited exemption)	Proof of employment
Cyprus	36	$21	Income (limited exemption)	$3,689 monthly
Czech Republic	12	$107	None	$5,644 in bank
Dominica	18	$800	Income; sales; import; capital gains; dividends	Proof of employment plus bank reference letter
Ecuador	24	$450	Income (limited exemption)	$1,275 monthly
Estonia	18	$106	Income (limited exemption)	$3,693 monthly
Georgia	12	$0	Income (limited exemption)	$2,000 monthly or $24,000 in bank
Germany	36	$185	Income (limited exemption); sales (limited exemption)	$9,400 annually

Country	Maximum stay (months)	Individual visa fee (USD)*	Tax exemptions?	Income requirements? (USD)*
Greece	36	$237	Income (limited exemption)	$3,688 monthly
Grenada	24	$1,500	Income	$37,000 annually
Hungary	24	$250	Income (limited exemption)	$2,108 monthly
Iceland	6	$88	Income	$7,196 monthly
Latvia	24	$190	Income	$3,012 monthly
Malaysia	24	$225	Income (limited exemption)	$24,000 annually
Malta	12	$317	Income	$34,151 annually
Mauritius	12+	$0	Income (limited exemption); sales (limited exemption)	$1,500 monthly
Mexico	48	$390	Income (limited exemption)	$2,600 monthly
Montserrat	12+	$500	Income; sales (limited exemption)	$70,000 annually
Namibia	6	$58	Income; social security	$2,000 monthly
Panama	18	$300	Income	$36,000 annually
Portugal	60	$164	Income (limited exemption)	$3,202 monthly
Romania	24	$0	Income	$3,477 monthly
Saint Lucia	12	$70	Income	Proof of employment
Seychelles	12	$47	Income	Proof of employment or business incorporation
Spain	60	$106	Income (limited exemption)	$2,459 monthly
Uruguay	6	$10	None	Proof of funds to cover stay
United Arab Emirates	24	$611	Income	$5,000 monthly

* Currency converted using xe.com on October 12, 2023.

Source: This table was compiled by the author from the digital nomad visa application data for each country.

Appendix B

The Traditional Model for Relocating Talent: A Summary of the Research

This appendix evaluates the traditional model for managing global talent in the pre-Covid era, that is, a model for relocating talent to locations where firms have offices. It also documents research insights on both the benefits and challenges of this approach.

The Traditional Relocation Model

While the Covid-19 pandemic may have thrust the global economy into a grand experiment with remote work, the fact remains that most companies have a physical office. This is true even among companies whose workers *can* do their work remotely. For these companies, talk of an all-remote model can seem light-years away from their reality. They continue to operate according to the traditional relocation model of attracting talent—that is, if a company wants to hire talented workers, it must either find those workers in its geographic area, find workers willing to move to that area, or entice them by funding that move from the company hiring budget. This model certainly has benefits, but it has challenges, too, as this appendix explores. And even companies whose feet remain firmly planted in physical offices can benefit from learning about how WFA companies work effectively, and how WFA policies can be incorporated into their management practice.

The Value of Traditional Relocation

As a child growing up in India, a part of my childhood was watching Bollywood movies. One common scene in these stories comes after the excitement of the wedding: a melodramatic sequence as the bride bids farewell to her childhood home and relocates to the groom's home (or *Sasural*), located in a faraway city. These scenes were always accompanied by a tearjerker of a song, evoking the sadness of a person leaving home, perhaps permanently.

For decades, employers around the world have followed a similar ritual, requiring their newly hired employees to live in the city, state, and country where the employer is located. For the millions of workers not originally from major hubs, this model has meant that to find work, particularly in certain high-paying and location-specific industries, they needed to pack up and move. For top talent, the cost of this relocation might be covered by their new employer, with companies competing with relocation benefits and expatriate packages, and an entire cottage industry of service providers emerging to help the workers with transportation and work visa services. It would not be an exaggeration to say that the relocation of talent orchestrated by companies, both within and between countries, has been the silent lifeblood that has helped multinational companies expand and maintain global operations.

The rationale of relocating employees for work lies in agglomeration economics: when multiple companies from one industry (or complementary industries—think, both car manufacturers and tire manufacturers) colocate, they can see positive effects.[1] But while talent is distributed everywhere, opportunity is not. Scholars like Harvard University's Edward Glaeser and the University of Toronto's Richard Florida have documented how career opportunities for skilled workers have been disproportionately concentrated within large cities and talent clusters.[2] While there are benefits to workers being clustered in certain regions, notably the sharing of knowledge within these so-called small-world networks, this unequal distribution of opportunity has left talented individuals living outside these clusters with few options but to leave their home regions and relocate.[3] Traditionally, organizations have played a central role in this process of relocation, requiring potential workers to move in order to access employment. This could take the form of a company requiring a new worker to move from their hometown to wherever the company was located or shifting an existing worker from one branch office location to another, even if that meant moving across the country or around the world.

Research, including mine, has shown the benefits of relocation for companies and individual workers alike. In particular, relocation creates value for organizations and individuals in three core ways: through knowledge transfer and recombination (that is, combining information in new ways to create new ideas), through the transfer of organizational norms and financial and social capital, and through opportunities for individual growth and skills development.

Knowledge Transfer and Recombination

The first way relocation creates value for companies and employees is by facilitating knowledge transfer between geographic regions. Individuals are more likely to exchange information when they are in close geographic or social proximity to one another. Economists Adam B. Jaffe (Brandeis University), Manuel Trajtenberg (Tel Aviv University), and Rebecca Henderson (Harvard University) have argued that information spillover was geographically localized—an argument later supported at the regional level in research done by Georgetown University's Paul Almeida, and Columbia Business School professor Bruce Kogut.[4] Other scholars, in contrast, have argued that social proximity can serve as a substitute for geographic proximity, making effective knowledge transfer possible even across large distances.[5] Some have even argued that the previous findings about geographic proximity and knowledge spillovers could be explained away with the simple fact that inventors working in a single industry and living in the same region were also likely to be in the same social and collaboration networks (in other words, their social proximity as much as their geographic proximity explained the knowledge transfer noted in previous research).[6] Through whichever pathway the knowledge is ultimately transferred, however, relocation serves to bring talented workers (and the knowledge they carry) to new locations, creating opportunities for new knowledge transfer.

This knowledge transfer can occur across borders as well as between regions within the same country. Taking the global perspective, geographically mobile workers can have a positive impact on business and innovation in both their destination and home countries, by transferring knowledge across borders and facilitating knowledge recombination. These mobile workers have been shown to have access to broader information networks than their nonmobile colleagues.[7] They can also bring contextual knowledge from their home countries to their destination countries, as was demonstrated in research I did with my former doctoral student and colleague, Boston College's Do Yoon Kim, on Chinese and Indian inventors in the US pharmaceutical industry.[8]

In our research, we found that Chinese and Indian inventors engaged in knowledge recombination by bringing their contextual knowledge of native herbal medicine to their western pharmaceutical companies for use in innovative ways.[9] We sought to assess the extent of this innovation by exploiting a natural experiment of the United States changing its H-1B visa numbers between the years 1999 and 2003, and found causal evidence that immigrant workers added value to top American companies via a significant increase in new herbal patent filings, as well as subsequent citations of those filings (see figure B-1).

As we began our research, Kim and I first focused on how knowledge was being transferred from the ancient books of Ayurveda and traditional Chinese medicine and used in patent application filings at the United States Patent and Trademark

FIGURE B-1

Knowledge transfer effect due to immigrant Chinese and Indian inventors

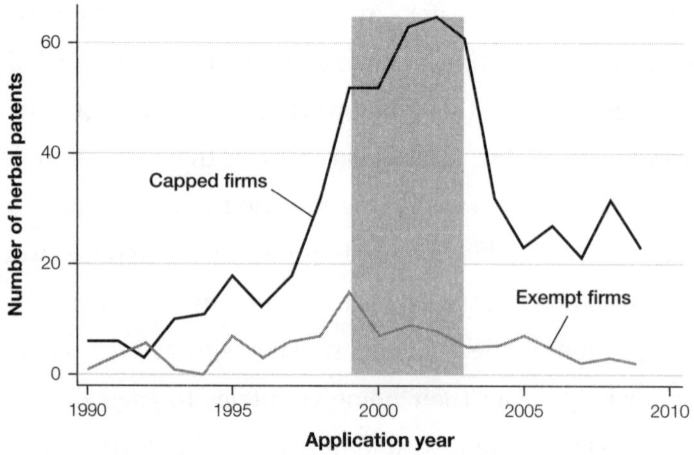

(a) All herbal patents

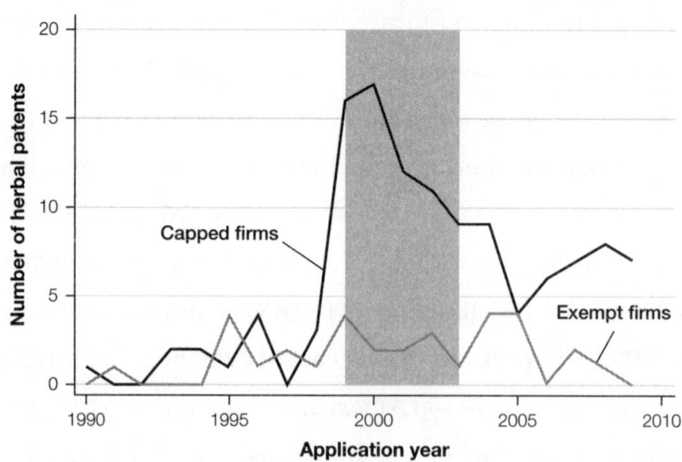

(b) Herbal patents by Chinese or Indians

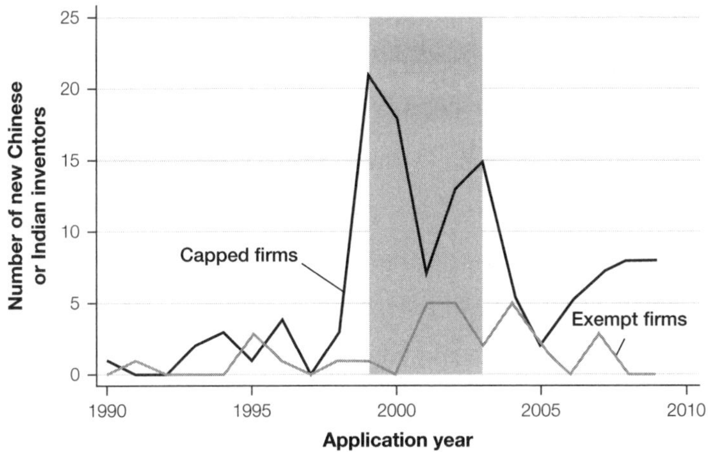

(c) New Chinese or Indian inventors

Source: Prithwiraj Choudhury and Do Yoon Kim, "The Ethnic Migrant Inventor Effect: Codification and Recombination of Knowledge across Borders," *Strategic Management Journal* 40, no. 2 (2019): 203–229.

Office. One example of this knowledge transfer pathway related to the anti-inflammatory properties of the Indian herb turmeric. This knowledge was transferred and codified by Hari P. Cohli, an Indian researcher working at the University of Mississippi. In an interview with me, Cohli revealed that he had absorbed this knowledge from attending religious sermons in India and had the opportunity to employ this knowledge while helping a friend (a doctor in the United States) treat and heal a patient who had faced amputation. Subsequently, Cohli and his friend filed for a patent related to this knowledge.

However, as Kim and I dug deeper, we discovered an interesting trend. Following the initial transfer of the knowledge from ancient medicinal textbooks to American pharmaceutical patents, the ancient knowledge was being *recombined* with more contemporary knowledge—specifically through adding synthetic compounds—to create brand-new medicinal formulations. Kim and I also found that this recombination of knowledge was being done primarily by mixed teams that included both ethnic migrant and local inventors, as well as by teams of local inventors by themselves (figure B-2). This finding revealed to us a profound insight related to the benefits of relocation: it not only leads to knowledge being shared between regions, but also spurs the creation of new knowledge. Kim and I realized, however, that this phenomenon is nothing new, and has in fact been playing out for centuries. One look at Americanized food like Chicago-style pizza or General Tso's chicken reveals the ways that the transfer and recombination of knowledge by migrants has resulted in new and valuable innovations.

FIGURE B-2

Knowledge recombination effect due to immigrant Chinese and Indian inventors

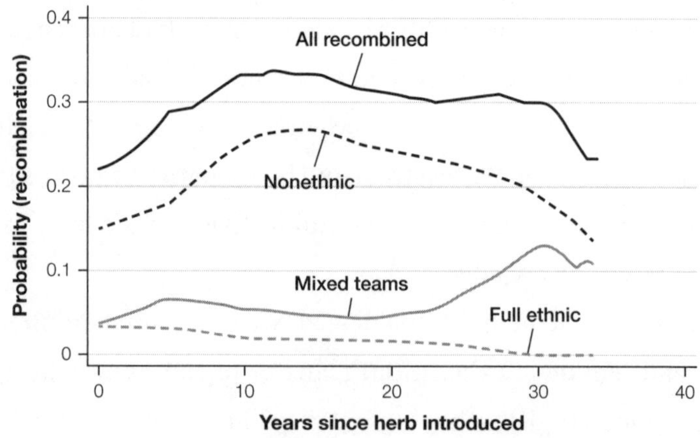

Source: Prithwiraj Choudhury and Do Yoon Kim, "The Ethnic Migrant Inventor Effect: Codification and Recombination of Knowledge across Borders," *Strategic Management Journal* 40, no. 2 (2019): 203–229.

In addition to collaborations between native and migrant inventors within a single country, recombination can also be activated through collaborations across borders. Workers who relocate between countries are more likely to facilitate these cross-border collaborations than their stationary colleagues.[10] This fact fits within research that teams will produce more and better innovation when they are made up of members with diverse expertise and backgrounds.[11] Scholars have also specifically found that teams comprised of members with international and/or cross-cultural experiences can yield positive results for innovation.[12]

In general, geographic relocation, and the individuals who choose to move, have repeatedly been shown to facilitate creativity and innovation.[13] A 2006 study by AnnaLee Saxenian, a professor at the University of California, Berkeley, revealed that when migrant workers returned home after working in Silicon Valley, they brought their overseas information and resources back to benefit burgeoning software development and technology markets in India, Taiwan, China, and Israel.[14] Much like our discussion of migrants recombining information to file new patents, the idea of migrant workers bringing new knowledge and bolstering innovation and creativity at their destination has occurred many times throughout history, from Russian scientists following the collapse of the Soviet Union, to German Jewish scientists exiled in the United States in the 1930s, and even Prussian-exiled Huguenots in the fifteenth century.[15]

In addition to fueling innovation in their destination countries, workers who relocate also bring beneficial knowledge back with them when they return to their home countries.[16] My research on return migrants (people who relocated to another country but later returned to their country of origin) at an Indian research and development (R&D) center of a *Fortune* 50 multinational company found that local employees with return migrant managers disproportionately filed more US patents than their counterparts with nonreturn migrant managers.[17] Since manager assignments were random in my research, I interpreted that there was a likely causal connection between the return managers' international experience and their direct reports' patent rates. I determined that the return migrant managers served as conduits of knowledge, moving key information from the company headquarters overseas to their local employees. This access to information had longer-term effects, too. Workers with return migrant managers not only had higher patenting rates in the time period I studied, but over time they evolved into the greatest contributors to innovation generated at this R&D center.

The knowledge transferred by workers as they relocate can also benefit economies on a macro scale. In research I conducted on ninety-five countries with economists Dany Bahar and Hillel Rapoport, the rise of migrant inventors in a given country paralleled a rise in patenting in industries in which the migrants' home countries specialized.[18] Research on the impact of foreign graduate students has similarly shown tangible contributions to innovation in their destination countries.[19]

Social Capital, Financial Capital, and Organizational Norms

Relocation of workers can also create value through other avenues, beyond access to knowledge and information. Access to financial capital, access to social capital, and understanding of organizational norms can all create value for relocated workers and the companies that employ them. Workers who have relocated can serve as conduits to networks their employers might not have access to otherwise, for collaborations, capital, and other resources.[20] For example, an engineer hired from a Taiwanese semiconductor company to an American tech firm will have a different professional network than his new colleagues in California. That network could come in handy if the new firm faces a challenge with its supply chain, or if it is considering marketing a new product to Taiwanese consumers. And even after moving on to another employer, the social access points these workers created could remain available to their former companies.[21]

Relocated workers can also create value when they establish their own entrepreneurial endeavors. Their influence on business and the economy can be found in research, whether they are starting companies after returning home, or in their destination country.[22] Research has also shown that migrants in the United States start their own businesses more than nonmigrants, with a quarter of new businesses being started by first-generation immigrants during the period of 2007–2012 (nearly half of which were founded in New York and California).[23] Economists Jackline Wahba and Yves Zenou found similar results in Egypt, with return migrant workers more likely to launch companies than their stationary peers.[24]

The geographic movement of workers also affects the economy through the movement of global financial capital. Research has shown that migrant population size is related to an increase in foreign direct investment both in and from the migrants' home country, as well as the exports sent.[25] Another study found that remittances sent abroad are associated with an increase in venture capital investment and businesses created in the migrants' home countries.[26]

The transfer of organizational norms—procedures, policies, or other structural standards—is another benefit worker relocation can provide. Given how much variety in prior experiences and cultural norms of employees exists within any given firm branch, not to mention on companywide teams, a company that can communicate its standards, culture, and procedures effectively is a company more likely to be successful in other locations, and more likely to be successful at educating teams with diverse backgrounds (cultural, geographic, and so forth).[27] Relocating workers can serve as conduits through which a company's standards and norms pass on to colleagues. Whether those workers are managers relocating from headquarters to other locations, workers moving temporarily to headquarters, or those changing locations throughout their careers—mobile workers enable the transfer of norms and standards for their respective employers.[28] Even when they leave a company and embark on other business ventures, as in Silicon Valley's migrant technology workers, workers with relocation experience can still bring their former employers' norms and standards to their new roles.[29]

Opportunities for Individuals

Worker relocation also provides value for the workers themselves, in several ways. It helps increase their value in the eyes of employers, and that perceived value can support their bargaining during negotiations.[30] Workers can also develop skills as a result of relocation, like communication or problem-solving abilities, which can aid them in their career advancement.[31] A good example is in the research I conducted on Indian bureaucrats with my colleague, University of Illinois Urbana-Champaign professor, Shinjinee Chattopadhyay. In that study, new Indian bureaucrats assigned randomly to difficult and remote locations progressed faster in their careers than their colleagues in more common locations, and we attributed their faster progress to the need to hone independent decision-making and problem-solving skills.[32] One of the bureaucrats I interviewed said that her first assignment to Karimnagar, a crime-prone district in South India, forced her to think outside the box. Rather than solely focusing on the local crime problem, she instead looked at alternative ways to gain the trust of local residents. So she launched a project to repair the village school and open a childcare center, and even employed family members of the insurgents responsible for much of the local crime issues at the two centers. The project was widely successful, and she confessed, "I would have never gained these problem-solving skills sitting in Bangalore."

Workers who relocate can also see wage benefits, as research has found that location alone can impact compensation; for instance, residing in ethnic enclaves or moving to cities may increase their wages.[33] The type of worker relocating can also affect this wage premium and/or career benefits; a 2011 study by Rutgers professor Jennifer Hunt found that highly skilled workers and permanent relocations resulted in higher wage gains than those enjoyed by other relocating workers.[34] This finding is echoed by work I did with McKinsey managers with relocation experience, who argued that establishing networks and resources in multiple locations had a positive effect on their career trajectories. One of the McKinsey consultants in my study shared with me that he was struggling to gain managerial opportunities within mature semiconductor clients while working in the highly competitive offices of the United States. However, when he took a leap of faith and relocated to the Japanese and Korean offices of the firm (despite not speaking the local languages), he was asked to step up and was given managerial opportunities in the then-fledgling semiconductor clients of the region. As the Korean semiconductor clients grew, so too did this individual's career.

Finally, relocation can also provide mobile workers with opportunities to access distant resources. Whether through cross-border mobility that leads to an enhanced knowledge base regarding international grants for academic research, or access to resource distributors (and therefore funding) at company headquarters, relocation can serve as an access point to novel resources for the workers who move.[35] Relocation can also give mobile entrepreneurs a leg up over rivals. A 2016 study by North Carolina State University professor Elena Kulchina found migrant access to novel capital resources (such as cheaper labor from their home countries) gave them a competitive advantage over rivals.[36]

The benefits of relocation are numerous for both companies and the mobile workers they employ. The transfer of knowledge among colleagues and in new business ventures, the positive impact on creativity and innovation, the access to novel networks and resources, as well as the impact on wages and skills, are but a few of the ways through which relocation can offer value. Yet despite these numerous benefits, there are also a multitude of frictions that can make relocation a challenging process.

The Challenges of Traditional Relocation

Workers who are required to relocate for work by their employers face challenges too—both constraints to relocation and economic and personal costs after the move. The Covid-19 pandemic shined a spotlight on some of these issues, and countless travel bans highlight the regulatory and personal frictions of relocating. It is important to understand these challenges prior to asking whether there is another way firms could be matched to geographically distant employees.

Through my long-standing research with multinational companies and workers who have relocated across continents and within regions of the country, and after a deep-dive review of several different streams of academic literature on geographic *immobility* (that is, factors that prevent people from engaging in mobility), I developed the ROPE framework: a conceptual model through which I organize the challenges workers and companies face when making the decision to relocate. Broadly speaking, the ROPE framework divides these relocation frictions into four categories (R, O, P, E): regulatory, occupational/organizational, personal, and economic/environmental.[37] In turn, each of these categories combine to make relocation more costly or prevent it altogether. (See table B-1 for more detail.)

Regulatory Frictions

Regulatory frictions are statutory limits to relocation that exist at the local, national, or international level. They can also include legislation designed to increase the challenges of relocation, regardless of whether those laws directly relate to geographic

TABLE B-1

Understanding geographic mobility frictions using the ROPE framework

Regulatory	Occupational/ organizational	Personal	Economic/ environmental
Visa regulations	Licensing requirements	Family obligations/ concerns	Information costs
Travel constrictions	Company restrictions	Emotional costs	Opportunity costs
Local/national/ international regulations		Cultural/social costs	Living expenses
Location-dependent benefits		Social attachments	Travel expenses

Source: Adapted from Prithwiraj Choudhury, "Make the Most of Your Relocation," *Harvard Business Review*, July–August 2020, 104–113.

mobility. Some examples of indirect regulations include visa regulation, household registration laws, tax laws, bankruptcy laws, and even child custody agreements.[38]

One example of regulatory frictions at the local and national level is the *hukou* system in China. As "a core Chinese socioeconomic institution," the *hukou* is a household registration system that citizens register with to determine their benefits based on their residency status as either rural (agricultural) or urban (nonagricultural); the system assigns them an area-specific designation.[39] While the *hukou* restrictions have been relaxed over the years, they had the effect of limiting migration from rural areas to urban cities, and to this day, dictate citizen access to public benefits such as housing subsidies, education, and health care.[40] Because the *hukou* restricted relocation into urban areas (which offered more opportunities for employment), it also served as a friction to geographic mobility.[41] While conducting research with Sercomm, a Taiwanese company that had set up R&D and manufacturing operations in China, I interviewed several migrant workers who relocated for a few months every year from their hometowns in the Chinese hinterland to the southern city of Suzhou. One of the reasons they were not able to relocate permanently to Suzhou was that their children could not be enrolled in local schools in Suzhou. As a result, the children were often left behind in their hometowns, being raised by the grandparents.

Visa regulations are a prime example of an international regulatory challenge for workers hoping to relocate. Visa regulations directly impede geographic mobility—with the potential to affect everyone from workers and academics, to scientists and students.[42] For those unable to secure a visa, relocation plans can be severely disrupted, and lead them to alter their planned destination, or force them to opt out and abandon moving altogether.[43] Along with my HBS colleague William Kerr, I studied how MobSquad, a Canadian startup founded by HBS alumnus Irfhan Rawji, had created a business model to help foreign workers who were denied visas or permanent residency in the United States relocate and work from Canada. As Kerr and I document, one MobSquad engineer had come to the United States after graduating from high school in his country at the age of twelve. At age sixteen, he enrolled at a US university and acquired degrees in math, physics, and computer science in three years. By age nineteen, he was employed at a medical tech company through the optional practical training (OPT) program, but he failed to get an H-1B visa and faced deportation after his OPT expired. MobSquad moved him to Calgary and helped him secure an accelerated Canadian work permit, and he continued working with the same US company—but while now living and paying taxes in Canada.

Other types of regulatory frictions that can prevent relocation include social benefits attached to a location, such as subsidized food benefits in the United States, as well as in India, and other location-based benefits such as healthcare access, housing vouchers, and public sector employment.[44] Access to these programs and benefits relies on an individual being physically present in a specific country or state, and the conditions to access benefits (income level, for example, or length of wait list) may differ from one place to another. Facing the loss of these benefits can add significant costs to relocation for workers, particularly if they are moving as a family or have relatively lower incomes.

Occupational/Organizational Frictions

Occupational and organizational frictions are job-specific challenges to relocation. A core example of an occupational friction is licensing requirements—for professions like lawyer, doctor, or beautician. Electricians, for example, must be licensed in the state where they work, and moving that licensure can take time and money, as well as often requiring them to retake their licensing exam. Organizational frictions are company-specific benefits and policies that make it harder for employees to change jobs, including health insurance, pensions, childcare benefits, or even noncompete clauses.

Some argue that occupational frictions like licensing were created to protect the public (for instance, doctors being certified to practice medicine and write prescriptions), and that therefore their benefits outweigh the costs.[45] Others, however, argue that restriction of relocation is the actual aim of these types of frictions.[46] The latter notion is supported by research on the effects of licensing on geographic mobility, which shows licensed professions face limitations to relocating both regionally and internationally.[47] A doctor licensed outside the United States, for instance, must repeat years of training and onerous testing requirements in order to re-earn the right to practice their chosen profession after moving to the United States, or must opt not to practice medicine, despite having already gone through the long years of study and practical training to earn their license. They may also choose not to migrate at all, deciding that being forced into such a choice outweighs any other benefits to relocating.

Organization-specific policies and norms can also prevent relocation—even when the limitations imposed are intended to dissuade mobility between companies (as opposed to between geographic locations).[48] Benefits like pensions or health insurance can be lost when workers relocate.[49] Predicaments like these can lead to a bureaucratic headache of transferring plans or researching care options, but they can also have tangible financial costs. Teachers who changed school districts even within a single state sometimes suffer significant loss in the value of their pension over the course of their career. Noncompete clauses are another organizational policy instrument that can affect whether and where a worker might relocate when considering a new job. Though some states have deemed them unenforceable, workers might opt *not* to take a job in a state that *does* enforce them.[50]

Personal Frictions

Personal frictions are intrinsic and extrinsic personal and cultural factors that can affect whether workers are willing and able to relocate. They can both affect workers asked to relocate by their current employer (meaning they may choose to quit rather than move) and limit opportunities for job seekers (meaning they may choose not to apply to otherwise appropriate roles located outside their preferred geography). The psychic costs of distance—homesickness, cultural distance, or distance from loved ones—can limit their willingness to relocate. Personal frictions can also include social factors, such as race in the United States impeding geographic mobility for Black workers, or caste in India limiting interstate mobility.[51] Familial obligations and other communal or group obligations can also restrict the ability of workers to relocate. For example, needing to retain access to family land or informal insurance networks can be a reason to remain in rural areas (or at least maintain a family presence in that area).[52] Family units might also make relocation decisions based on major life events (marriage, childbirth, and so forth), or in hopes of maximizing income. These factors may lead one person to relocate to find work while others stay behind, or lead children to remain with grandparents while working-age individuals relocate.[53] Such decisions are also affected by gender dynamics (which often result in favoring the husband's income, and therefore, employment location), increased moving costs for dual-income households, and the extent of a family's embeddedness within a community.[54]

Beyond familial concerns, homesickness and community involvement (or, social embeddedness) can make workers wary of relocation.[55] The psychic costs of these frictions have been shown to affect the moving decisions of everyone from CEOs and entrepreneurs, to technical workers and other workers.[56] These costs can factor into policymaking, both for those hoping to provide opportunities and support to struggling communities and those hoping to encourage workers to relocate toward locations with more opportunities.[57] Firms can also put policies into place to minimize the effects of homesickness on their workers who do relocate, as research has shown that access to flexible vacation time and other paid leave can do just that.[58]

Another type of personal friction of note is cultural distance, or "the intercultural differences that complicate interactions between individuals in distant locations."[59] Cultural distance can include financial and bureaucratic differences, as well as differences in leadership, work-life balance, and language perceptions.[60] It can detrimentally impact migrant workers adjusting to new environments and discourage relocating.[61]

Practically speaking, personal frictions are often the most emotionally challenging parts of relocation. For a worker considering a distant move, and especially a move around the world, there are a lot of factors that might make them reluctant to make such a dramatic change. Being far away from friends and family, both in terms of material support like grandma or grandpa helping with childcare and in terms of the comfort you feel around friends, can be a major stumbling block. Those facing life in a new culture or needing to operate in their non-native language have additional challenges. Even things as simple as favorite foods, spices, or the ability to watch your favorite sports team can all contribute to a sense of loss for workers considering relocation. A biography of

Srinivasa Ramanujan documents how at the end of a long visit to England, the mathematician longed for the familiar sounds and smells of his native hometown and arguably faced a mental breakdown as a result.[62] Noted historian Sunil Amrith writes about migrants from South Asia using recorded cassettes to transport the voices of loved ones across geography.[63] Even in the age of direct flights, relocated workers face homesickness and emotional challenges. Along with my collaborators Caroline Elkins and Tarun Khanna, I interviewed Chinese migrants building and operating a modern railway in Kenya. One of the relocated workers described how the one-child policy of China has made it harder for Chinese migrants to take care of elderly parents (because they have no siblings to share the load), prompting many to either cut short their employment-based relocation, or consider not relocating for work.

These challenges compound for families seeking to move, as a trailing spouse may or may not be giving up their career (regulatory frictions can come into play here, too) to make the move, and displacing children from their schools, friends, and activities can also impose a tangible cost on the family unit. All these challenges must be weighed when workers move for work.

Economic/Environmental Frictions

The last category of frictions is economic and environmental. These types of challenges include the financial costs of relocation (such as moving, housing, commuting, and so forth), the information costs of learning the lay of the land and opportunities of a new location; they also include the effects of macro trends like natural disasters, pandemics, and climate change.

Financial costs to moving can represent a significant impediment to relocation for workers. Receiving a higher income is often a key incentive for workers to relocate, and the likelihood of receiving a premium wage in the new location plays a major role in whether or not workers opt to move.[64] On the other hand, the higher the costs associated with moving, the less likely workers are to relocate.[65] This holds true even for workers who would likely receive a premium wage in another location, and particularly for workers balancing family considerations.[66]

Other costs associated with the new destination can also deter potential mobile workers. For example, the potential higher cost of living—including housing and commuting—serve as potential barriers to relocation.[67] The same holds true for costs related to offloading a home in the current location prior to moving, such as losing money on the sale or a lengthy sale process.[68] Beyond those challenges, the potential information costs of being able to identify opportunities in the destination market can hinder relocation.[69] Information costs can be mitigated, however, with better transportation infrastructure to reduce the impact of distance on information flow, and improved access to job opportunity information and social networks in the destination location.[70]

Ultimately, relocation is expensive, and so is living in the cities where the highest-paying jobs are located. Though for some workers, the potential income increase they receive from relocating will outweigh those costs, for others, it may not. For families, especially, this can lead to split mobility decisions, where some of a family unit (generally the breadwinner) will travel to a high-cost, high-pay environment to work, while the rest of the family remains in their lower-cost hometown. Though this is a way to maximize economic benefits, it comes along with additional costs as well, particularly in terms of interpersonal relationships and emotional health.

Environmental frictions can be local, regional, or international. These barriers, including pandemics (such as Covid-19), can also come with regulatory responses that limit (via travel bans), or encourage (by incentivizing people to move away from an area) relocation.[71] Researchers have shown the effects of climate change on whether and how people relocate can range from forcing long-term abandonment of a region, to short moves followed by a return, to remaining in place despite a changed landscape, or even developing new patterns of seasonal migration.[72]

Considering WFA as an Alternative to the Relocation Model

Although the benefits to geographic mobility can be plentiful for both employers and employees, there are significant challenges to relocation that firms and workers should consider. These frictions as outlined in the ROPE framework—regulatory, occupational/organizational, personal, and economic/environmental—can seriously impede, or altogether prevent, workers from engaging in mobility. Given these challenges, managers should consider an alternative work arrangement for distant workers. Instead of requiring workers to relocate permanently, why not require them to travel for short periods of time? Better still, why not let them choose where to live and work from anywhere?

Research into the Popularity of Hybridity

Why has hybrid work gained in popularity and replaced in-person work so quickly? There are two competing forces at play when designing an optimal work arrangement. The first force is flexibility—awarded in geographic flexibility, temporal flexibility, and a reduction in commute time and distance—that tends to create positive productivity effects. The second force is isolation—manifested as social and professional isolation, and lack of organizational attachment—that can instead create negative productivity effects. For organizations deciding whether WFA is right for them and how to design the optimal hybrid work arrangement, striking the balance between these competing factors is key to determining what their new work arrangement should be. One way to visualize this balance is shown in figure B-3, relating the fraction of in-person days to worker productivity.

As you can see, both intensive in-person work arrangements (such as five days in-person every week of the month) and intensive remote work arrangements (such as no in-person days) have their downsides. The sweet spot lies in the middle, offering the benefits of flexibility while mitigating the challenges of isolation. This ideal middle ground is what well-designed hybrid work represents. Survey findings among American workers echo this sentiment, showing that an approximately half hybrid schedule is the sweet spot where the desires of workers and desires of employers converge.[73]

For a real-world application of this theory, I worked with coauthors Tarun Khanna (HBS), Christos Makridis (Stanford), and

FIGURE B-3

Effects of flexibility and isolation on productivity in hybrid models

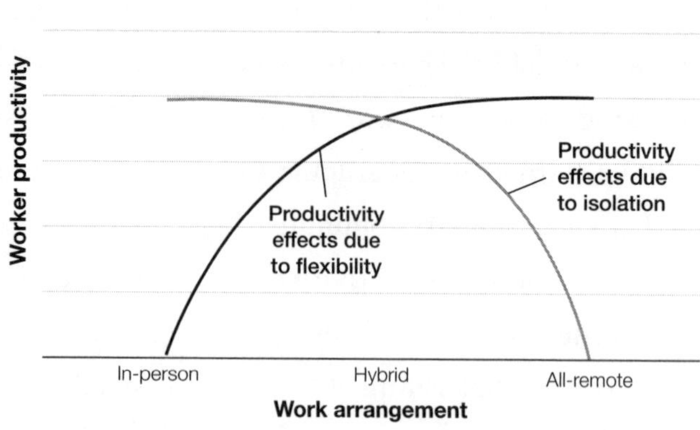

Source: Prithwiraj Choudhury, "TCS: From Physical Offices to Borderless Work," teaching note 623-037 (Boston: Harvard Business School, 2023): 7.

Kyle Schirmann (HBS) to run a randomized controlled test on this very issue at BRAC, a global international development organization headquartered in Bangladesh.[74] As the organization returned to the office following the 2020 Covid shutdowns, they intended to implement a hybrid schedule, in order to keep office density low. We worked with the organization to randomize the in-office schedule over a period of nine weeks, which then allowed us to find causal relationships between amount of in-office time and measures like productivity, performance, and colleague communication. We found that across metrics, workers who were in the office for an intermediate amount of time (23–40 percent of the time, or about two days per week) reported greater job satisfaction and work-life balance, compared to their counterparts with either lower OR higher amounts of in-office time. The intermediate group was also found to have a greater volume of colleague emails, covering a greater breadth of topics in those communications, and containing more novel content than the emails of their counterparts. We also checked on the experiment participants again six months later, and found that some of these workers, especially managers themselves, received higher ratings in performance reviews when in the intermediate group. These findings clearly show that a hybrid approach can be the best of both worlds. In a related, contemporaneous study, Nicholas Bloom and colleagues report that hybrid working improved job satisfaction and reduced quit rates by one-third, with no drop in productivity.[75] It is also important to remember that hybrid models can come in different forms, ranging from weekly hybrid to quarterly hybrid (see chapter 6).

Notes

Introduction

1. John S. Niles, *Beyond Telecommuting: A New Paradigm for the Effect of Telecommunications on Travel,* no. DOE/ER-0626, USDOE Office of Energy Research, Washington, DC, 1994, https://doi.org/10.2172/10188598; Pamela Hinds and Sara Kiesler, eds., *Distributed Work* (Cambridge, MA: MIT Press, 2002).

2. Prithwiraj Choudhury, Barbara Z. Larson, and Cirrus Foroughi, "Is It Time to Let Employees Work from Anywhere?," hbr.org, August 14, 2019, https://hbr.org/2019/08/is-it-time-to-let-employees-work-from-anywhere.

Chapter 1

1. "GitLab Net Worth 2021–2023 | GTLB," Macrotrends, https://www.macrotrends.net/stocks/charts/GTLB/gitlab/net-worth.

2. Jose Maria Barrero, Nicholas Bloom, and Steven J. Davis, "Why Working from Home Will Stick," working paper 28731, National Bureau of Economic Research, April 2021, https://www.nber.org/papers/w28731.

3. Alana Semuels, "Fully Flexible Companies Are Growing More Quickly," *Time,* July 18, 2023, https://time.com/6294640/remote-work-winning/.

4. "The Flex Report: Job Growth Edition, July 2023," Flex Index, July 2023, https://www.flex.scoopforwork.com/reports/job-growth.

5. Arpit Gupta, Vrinda Mittal, and Stijn Van Nieuwerburgh, "Work from Home and the Office Real Estate Apocalypse," working paper 30526, National Bureau of Economic Research, September 2022, https://www.nber.org/papers/w30526.

6. Arjun Ramani and Nicholas Bloom, "The Donut Effect of Covid-19 on Cities," working paper 28876, National Bureau of Economic Research, May 2021, https://www.nber.org/papers/w28876.

7. Yuye Ding and Mark Shuai Ma, "Return-to-Office Mandates," SSRN, January 18, 2024, https://papers.ssrn.com/abstract 4675401.

8. David H. Hsu and Prasanna B. Tambe, "Remote Work and Job Applicant Diversity: Evidence from Technology Startups," *Management Science* (April 15, 2024), https://pubsonline.informs.org/doi/abs/10.1287/mnsc.2022.03391.

9. Prithwiraj Choudhury and Malini Sen, "TCS: From Physical Offices to Borderless Work," Case 621-081 (Boston: Harvard Business School, 2021).

10. "Family Member Employment within a U.S. Embassy or Consulate," US Department of State, https://www.state.gov/global-community-liaison-office/family-member-employment/overseas-family-member-employment/family-member-employment-within-a-u-s-embassy-or-consulate/.

11. Prithwiraj Choudhury, William R. Kerr, and Susie L. Ma, "MobSquad," Case 821-010 (Boston: Harvard Business School, 2020).

12. Caroline M. Elkins, Tarun Khanna, and Joyce J. Kim, "Andela: Africa's AWS for Talent," Case 321-113 (Boston: Harvard Business School, January 2021).

13. Maxine Williams, "Embracing Change through Inclusion: Meta's 2022 Diversity Report," Meta, July 19, 2022, https://about.fb.com/news/2022/07/metas-diversity-report-2022/.

14. Imani Dunbar, "With Uncertainty on the Horizon, Remote Roles Have an Additional Value: Workforce Diversity," LinkedIn, November 3, 2022, https://www.linkedin.com/business/talent/blog/talent-acquisition/with-uncertainty-on-the-horizon-remote-roles-have-an-additional-value-workforce-diversity.

15. Suhani Jalota and Lisa Ho, "What Works for Her? How Work-from-Home Jobs Affect Female Labor Force Participation in Urban India," SSRN, January 4, 2024, https://papers.ssrn.com/sol3/papers.cfm?abstract_id=4739387.

16. "U.S. Patent and Trademark Office Ranks #1 in Best Places to Work in the Federal Government," December 18, 2013, https://www.uspto.gov/about-us/news-updates/us-patent-and-trademark-office-ranks-1-best-places-work-federal-government, accessed November 2016.

17. Prithwiraj Choudhury, Tarun Khanna, and Sarah Mehta, "The Future of Patent Examination at the USPTO," Case 617-027 (Boston: Harvard Business School, 2017).

18. Thomaz Teodorovicz, Prithwiraj Choudhury, and Evan Starr, "Location Specificity and Geographic Competition for Remote Workers," *Organization Science* (May 7, 2024), https://pubsonline.informs.org/doi/abs/10.1287/orsc.2023.17712.

19. Nicholas Bloom et al., "Does Working from Home Work? Evidence from a Chinese Experiment," *The Quarterly Journal of Economics* 130, no. 1 (February 2015): 165–218, https://doi.org/10.1093/qje/qju032.

20. Natalia Emanuel and Emma Harrington, "Working Remotely? Selection, Treatment, and the Market for Remote Work," *American Economic Journal: Applied Economics* 16, no. 4 (2024): 528–559, DOI: 10.1257/app.20230376.

21. Abigail Johnson Hess, "Here's How Much Every Inch of Apple's New $5 Billion Campus Cost to Build," CNBC, October 9, 2017, https://www.cnbc.com/2017/10/09/how-much-every-inch-of-apples-new-5-billion-campus-cost-to-build.html.

22. Prithwiraj Choudhury, "Our Work-from-Anywhere Future," *Harvard Business Review*, November–December 2020, 58–67.

23. "The Costs and Benefits of Hybrid Work," Global Workplace Analytics, https://globalworkplaceanalytics.com/resources/costs-benefits.

24. Choudhury, "Our Work-from-Anywhere Future."

25. "Greenhouse Gas Emissions from a Typical Passenger Vehicle," US Environmental Protection Agency, January 12, 2016, https://www.epa.gov/greenvehicles/greenhouse-gas-emissions-typical-passenger-vehicle.

26. "USPTO Telework Annual Report 2015," US Patent and Trademark Office, https://www.uspto.gov/sites/default/files/documents/TeleworkAnnualReport2015-508.pdf.

27. "Conrad 30 Waiver Program," US Citizenship and Immigration Services, May 15, 2020, https://www.uscis.gov/working-in-the-united-states/students-and-exchange-visitors/conrad-30-waiver-program.

28. Prithwiraj Choudhury, Emma Salomon, and Brittany Logan, "Tulsa Remote: Moving Talent to Middle America," Case 621-048 (Boston: Harvard Business School, 2020).

Chapter 2

1. Cor Verdouw et al., "Digital Twins in Smart Farming," *Agricultural Systems* 189 (April 2021): 103046, https://doi.org/10.1016/j.agsy.2020.103046.

2. Mark Chillingworth, "Digital Twin Enables Customer Experience Renaissance at Rome Airport," Diginomica, August 31, 2022, https://diginomica.com/digital-twin-enables-customer-experience-renaissance-rome-airport.

3. "From Digital Twin to Improved Patient Experience," Siemens Healthineers, September 11, 2018, https://www.siemens-healthineers.com/perspectives/mso-digital-twin-mater.html.

4. Mike Geyer, "BMW Group Starts Global Rollout of NVIDIA Omniverse," NVIDIA, March 21, 2023, https://blogs.nvidia.com/blog/2023/03/21/bmw-group-nvidia-omniverse/.

5. Prithwiraj Choudhury and Susie Ma, "Unilever: Remote Work in Manufacturing," Case 622-030 (Boston: Harvard Business School, 2022).

6. Leanne Birch, "EU/EEA | Social Security—A1s for Teleworkers / Workations," LinkedIn, July 19, 2022, https://www.linkedin.com/pulse/eueea-social-security-a1s-teleworkers-workations-leanne-birch/.

7. "INTM264435—Non-Residents Trading in the UK: Permanent Establishment: Domestic and Treaty Law: Fixed Place of Business," HMRC Internal Manual, GOV.UK, April 9, 2016, https://www.gov.uk/hmrc-internal-manuals/international-manual/intm264435.

8. Julia Hauck, "Employers of Record: The Solution for a Compliant 'Work-from-Anywhere' Future?," MasterCourse on Human Resources and Global Mobility, Erasmus University, January 10, 2021, https://feibv.nl/wp-content/uploads/2022/06/Employers-of-Record-The-Solution-for-a-Compliant-Work-from-Anywhere-Future_Hauck_final.pdf.

9. "What Is a PEO? Exploring Its Role in HR Outsourcing," SHRM, https://www.shrm.org/topics-tools/tools/hr-answers/peo-advantages-disadvantages.

10. Pieter Haeck and Gian Volpicelli, "Portugal's Digital Nomad Bubble Poised to Pop," *POLITICO*, January 1, 2023, https://www.politico.eu/article/portugal-digital-nomads-bubble-gentrification/.

11. "Live, Work, and Explore in Costa Rica," Essential Costa Rica, https://www.visitcostarica.com/en/costa-rica/digital-nomads.

12. "Life Works Here," Finding NWA, https://findingnwa.com/incentive/.

13. Cailin Crowe, "Topeka, KS Extends Remote Worker Relocation Program," Smart Cities Dive, September 15, 2020, https://.smartcitiesdive.com/news/topeka-kansas-pay-remote-workers-10k-pandemic/585196/.

14. "Get Paid $12,000 + Free Outdoor Recreation," Ascend West Virginia, https://ascendwv.com/.

15. Prithwiraj Choudhury, Brittany Logan, and Emma Salomon, "Tulsa Remote: Moving Talent to Middle America," Case 621-048 (Boston: Harvard Business School, 2020, rev. 2023).

16. "Lessons from a Leading Remote Work Incentive in Tulsa, Oklahoma," Economic Innovation Group, November 2021, https://eig.org/tulsa-remote.

17. "The Seychelles Workcation Retreat Program," Seychelles Electronic Border System, https://seychelles.govtas.com/workcation;

"Costa Rica Rentista Visa for Digital Nomads," VisaGuide.World, https://visaguide.world/digital-nomad-visa/costa-rica/; "e-Residency vs Digital Nomad Visa," Republic of Estonia E-Residency, January 3, 2023, https://www.e-resident.gov.ee/nomadvisa/.

18. "Portugal D7 Residence Visa," Clara Silva da Costa Law Office, 2023, August 14, 2023, https://www.portuguese-nationality.com/residency/the-d7-visa-portugal.

19. Sundar Pichai, "A Hybrid Approach to Work," Google, May 5, 2021, https://blog.google/inside-google/life-at-google/hybrid-approach-work/.

20. Stephanie Chan, "Cisco's Corporate Nomads Take Hybrid Work to the Next Level in Venice, Italy," Cisco, April 13, 2022, https://newsroom.cisco.com/c/r/newsroom/en/us/a/y2022/m04/cisco-corporate-nomads-take-hybrid-work-to-the-next-level-in-venice-italy.html.

Chapter 3

1. Wendy Naugle, "Apple CEO Tim Cook Expects a Post-Pandemic Return to the Office: 'I Can't Wait,'" *People,* March 18, 2021, https://people.com/human-interest/apple-ceo-tim-cook-expects-return-to-office-post-pandemic/.

2. Catherine Durnell Cramton, "The Mutual Knowledge Problem and Its Consequences for Dispersed Collaboration," *Organization Science* 12, no. 3 (June 2001): 346–371, https://doi.org/10.1287/orsc.12.3.346.10098; Richard L. Daft and Robert H. Lengel, "Organizational Information Requirements, Media Richness and Structural Design," *Management Science* 32, no. 5 (1986): 554–571, https://doi.org/10.1287/mnsc.32.5.554.

3. Martine R. Haas and Morten T. Hansen, "Different Knowledge, Different Benefits: Toward a Productivity Perspective on Knowledge Sharing in Organizations," *Strategic Management Journal* 28, no. 11 (2007): 1133–1153, https://doi.org/10.1002/smj.631.

4. Prithwiraj Choudhury and Emma Salomon, "GitLab and the Future of All-Remote Work (A)," Case 620-066 (Boston: Harvard Business School, 2020).

5. For examples, see Anders Edström and Jay R. Galbraith, "Transfer of Managers as a Coordination and Control Strategy in Multinational Organizations," *Administrative Science Quarterly* 22, no. 2 (1977): 248–263, https://doi.org/10.2307/2391959; Pankaj Ghemawat, "Distance Still Matters: The Hard Reality of Global Expansion," *Harvard Business Review,* September 2001; Geert Hofstede, *Culture's Consequences: International Differences in Work-Related Values,* vol. 5, Cross-Cultural Research and Methodology Series (Beverly Hills, CA: Sage Publications, 1980);

Srilata Zaheer, "Overcoming the Liability of Foreignness," *Academy of Management Journal* 38, no. 2 (1995): 341–363, https://doi.org/10.2307/256683.

6. Thomas J. Allen, *Managing the Flow of Technology: Technology Transfer and the Dissemination of Technological Information within the R&D Organization* (Cambridge, MA: MIT Press, 1977).

7. Prithwiraj Choudhury, Francesca Gino, and Jeffrey Huizinga, "Doist: Building the Future of Asynchronous Work," Case 621-096 (Boston: Harvard Business School, 2021).

8. The author acknowledges the help of Rebecca Hinds, a doctoral student at Stanford, in drafting this subsection.

9. Teresa M. Amabile, "A Model of Creativity and Innovation in Organizations," *Research in Organizational Behavior* 10, no. 1 (1988): 123–167, https://web.mit.edu/curhan/www/docs/Articles/15341_Readings/Group_Performance/Amabile_A_Model_of_CreativityOrg.Beh_v10_pp123-167.pdf.

10. Anne-Laure Fayard and Anca Metiu, "The Role of Writing in Distributed Collaboration," *Organization Science* 25, no. 5 (2014): 1391–1413, https://pubsonline.informs.org/doi/10.1287/orsc.2013.0893.

11. Peter A. Heslin, "Better Than Brainstorming? Potential Contextual Boundary Conditions to Brainwriting for Idea Generation in Organizations," *Journal of Occupational and Organizational Psychology* 82, no. 1 (2009): 129–145, https://doi.org/10.1348/096317908X285642.

12. Sergio Rizzuti and Luigi De Napoli, "Interactive Freehand Sketching as the Means for Online Communication of Design Intent in Conceptual Design Conducted by Brainwriting," *International Journal on Interactive Design and Manufacturing (IJIDeM)* 15, no. 8 (2021): 143–149, https://link.springer.com/article/10.1007/s12008-020-00745-x.

13. Jin K. Hammick and Moon J. Lee, "Do Shy People Feel Less Communication Apprehension Online? The Effects of Virtual Reality on the Relationship between Personality Characteristics and Communication Outcomes," *Computers in Human Behavior* 33 (April 2014): 302–310, https://doi.org/10.1016/j.chb.2013.01.046.

14. Benjamin Laker et al., "The Surprising Impact of Meeting-Free Days," *MIT Sloan Management Review*, January 18, 2022, https://sloanreview.mit.edu/article/the-surprising-impact-of-meeting-free-days/.

15. Forrest Briscoe, "From Iron Cage to Iron Shield? How Bureaucracy Enables Temporal Flexibility for Professional Service Workers," *Organization Science* 18, no. 2 (April 2007): 297–314, https://doi.org/10.1287/orsc.1060.0226.

16. Anna Brown, "What Is Flexible Work?," Future Forum, May 5, 2022, https://futureforum.com/2022/05/05/what-is-flexible-work/.

17. Gunnar Newquist and R. Allen Gardner, "Reconsidering Food Reward, Brain Stimulation, and Dopamine: Incentives Act Forward," *The American Journal of Psychology* 128, no. 4 (2015): 431–444, https://scholarlypublishingcollective.org/uip/ajp/article-abstract/128/4/431/258134/Reconsidering-Food-Reward-Brain-Stimulation-and.

18. B. F. Skinner, "On the Conditions of Elicitation of Certain Eating Reflexes," *Proceedings of the National Academy of Sciences* 16, no. 6 (June 15, 1930): 433–438, https://doi.org/10.1073/pnas.16.6.433.

19. Paul M. Leonardi, Tsedal B. Neeley, and Elizabeth M. Gerber, "How Managers Use Multiple Media: Discrepant Events, Power, and Timing in Redundant Communication," *Organization Science* 23, no. 1 (April 2011): 98–117, https://doi.org/10.1287/orsc.1110.0638.

20. Rob Cross et al., "How to Fix Collaboration Overload," hbr.org, December 9, 2022, https://hbr.org/2022/12/how-to-fix-collaboration-overload.

21. Gloria Mark, Daniela Gudith, and Ulrich Klocke, "The Cost of Interrupted Work: More Speed and Stress," *CHI '08: Proceedings of the SIGCHI Conference on Human Factors in Computing Systems*, 107–110, https://www.ics.uci.edu/~gmark/chi08-mark.pdf.

22. Marissa King and Balázs Kovács, "Research: We're Losing Touch with Our Networks," hbr.org, February 12, 2021, https://hbr.org/2021/02/research-were-losing-touch-with-our-networks.

23. Longqui Yang et al., "The Effects of Remote Work on Collaboration among Information Workers," *Nature Human Behaviour* 6 (2022): 164, https://doi.org/10.1038/s41562-021-01228-z.

24. Hugh Son, "Citigroup CEO Jane Fraser Calls for Zoom-Free Fridays and New Bank Holiday as Pandemic Fatigue Grows," CNBC, March 23, 2021, https://www.cnbc.com/2021/03/23/citigroup-ceo-jane-fraser-calls-for-zoom-free-fridays.html; Jason Fried, "An Office with 'Library Rules,'" *Signal v. Noise*, December 10, 2012, https://signalvnoise.com/posts/3357-an-office-with-ldquolibrary-rulesrdquo.

25. John Rampton, "Time Blocking Tips Top Experts and Scientists Use to Increase Productivity," *Entrepreneur*, April 16, 2019, https://www.entrepreneur.com/living/time-blocking-tips-top-experts-and-scientists-use-to/332290.

26. Leah Fessler, "Completing This 30-Minute Exercise Makes Teams Less Anxious and More Productive," Quartz, August 9, 2017, https://qz.com/1046131/writing-a-user-manual-at-work-makes-teams-less-anxious-and-more-productive.

Chapter 4

1. “Satya Nadella Talks to Adam Grant about the Future of Work,” Microsoft, n.d., https://www.microsoft.com/en-us/worklab/satya-nadella-talks-to-adam-grant-about-the-future-of-work.

2. Charles C. Manz and Henry P. Sims Jr., “Vicarious Learning: The Influence of Modeling on Organizational Behavior,” *Academy of Management Review* 6, no. 1 (1981): 105–113; Albert Bandura and Richard H. Walters, *Social Learning Theory*, vol. 1 (Englewood Cliffs, NJ: Prentice Hall, 1977).

3. Prithwiraj Choudhury and Emma Salomon, “GitLab and the Future of All-Remote Work (A),” Case 620-066 (Boston: Harvard Business School, 2020).

4. Jasmina Chauvin, Prithwiraj Choudhury, and Tommy Pan Fang, “Working Around the Clock: Temporal Distance, Intrafirm Communication, and Time Shifting of the Employee Workday,” *Organization Science* (May 30, 2024), https://pubsonline.informs.org/doi/10.1287/orsc.2023.17558.

5. As Michael Polanyi theorized, there is also knowledge that is tacit and noncodifiable: for instance, the fingers of the surgeon or the feet of the dancer might know moves that cannot be written down. Michael Polanyi, *The Tacit Dimension* (Garden City, NY: Doubleday, 1966).

6. Martine R. Haas and Morten T. Hansen, “Different Knowledge, Different Benefits: Toward a Productivity Perspective on Knowledge Sharing in Organizations,” *Strategic Management Journal* 28, no. 11 (2007): 1133–1153, https://doi.org/10.1002/smj.631.

7. Haas and Hansen, “Different Knowledge, Different Benefits.”

8. Morten T. Hansen and Martine R. Haas, “Competing for Attention in Knowledge Markets: Electronic Document Dissemination in a Management Consulting Company,” *Administrative Science Quarterly* 46, no. 1 (2001): 1–28, https://journals.sagepub.com/doi/10.2307/2667123.

9. ”GitLab Handbook,” GitLab, https://about.gitlab.com/handbook/.

10. For examples of previous academic study of stigmergy in biology, see Pierre P. Grassé, “La theorie de la stigmergie: Essai d’interpretation du comportement des termites constructeurs,” *Insectes Sociaux* 6 (1959): 41–81; E. Bonabeau, M. Dorigo, and G. Theraulaz, “Inspiration for Optimization from Social Insect Behaviour,” *Nature* 406, no. 6791 (July 2000): 39–42; Francis Heylighen, “Stigmergy as a Universal Coordination Mechanism I: Definition and Components,” *Cognitive Systems Research* 38 (2016): 4–13; Francis Heylighen, “Stigmergy as a Universal Coordination Mechanism II: Varieties and Evolution,” *Cognitive Systems Research*

38 (2016): 50–59. For discussions of stigmergy in computer-supported collaboration and open-source software development, see Matthijs den Besten, Jean-Michel Dalle, and Fabrice Galia, "The Allocation of Collaborative Efforts in Open-Source Software," *Information Economics and Policy* 20, no. 4 (December 2008): 316–322; James Howison and Kevin Crowston, "Collaboration through Open Superposition: A Theory of the Open Source Way," *MIS Quarterly* 38, no. 1 (March 2014): 29–50; Mark Elliott, "Stigmergic Collaboration: A Framework for Understanding and Designing Mass Collaboration," in *Mass Collaboration and Education*, ed. U. Cress, H. Jeong, and J. Moskaliuk, vol. 16, *Computer-Supported Collaborative Learning Series* (Cham, Switzerland: Springer International Publishing, 2016), 65–84.

11. David J. T. Sumpter and Madeleine Beekman, "From Nonlinearity to Optimality: Pheromone Trail Foraging by Ants," *Animal Behaviour* 66, no. 2 (August 2003): 273–280.

12. Prithwiraj Choudhury and Thorsten Grohsjean, "Stigmergy and Knowledge Sharing in All-Remote and Hybrid-Remote Organizations," unpublished manuscript, 2021.

13. Prithwiraj Choudhury and Emma Salomon, video supplement to "GitLab and the Future of All-Remote Work (A)," Case 620-066 (Boston: Harvard Business School, 2020).

Chapter 5

1. Andy Serwer and Dylan Croll, "Jamie Dimon Sounds Off on . . . Almost Everything: Morning Brief," Yahoo Finance, August 13, 2022, https://ca.finance.yahoo.com/news/jamie-dimon-sounds-off-morning-brief-110044236.html.

2. Nicholas Bloom et al., "Does Working from Home Work? Evidence from a Chinese Experiment," *The Quarterly Journal of Economics* 130, no. 1 (February 2015): 205.

3. Caroline A. Bartel, Amy Wrzesniewski, and Batia M. Wiesenfeld, "Knowing Where You Stand: Physical Isolation, Perceived Respect, and Organizational Identification among Virtual Employees," *Organization Science* 23, no. 3 (June 2012): 743–757; Timothy D. Golden, John F. Veiga, and Richard N. Dino, "The Impact of Professional Isolation on Teleworker Job Performance and Turnover Intentions: Does Time Spent Teleworking, Interacting Face-to-Face, or Having Access to Communication-Enhancing Technology Matter?," *Journal of Applied Psychology* 93, no. 6 (2008): 1412–1421; Cecily D. Cooper and Nancy B. Kurland, "Telecommuting,

Professional Isolation, and Employee Development in Public and Private Organizations," *Journal of Organizational Behavior* 23, no. 4 (June 2002): 511–532.

4. Prithwiraj Choudhury et al., "Is Hybrid Work the Best of Both Worlds? Evidence from a Field Experiment," *The Review of Economics and Statistics* (2024): 1–24, https://doi.org/10.1162/rest_a_01428.

5. Gary Johns, "Presenteeism in the Workplace: A Review and Research Agenda," *Journal of Organizational Behavior* 31, no. 4 (2010): 519–542.

6. Myungjung Kwon and So Hee Jeon, "Do Leadership Commitment and Performance-Oriented Culture Matter for Federal Teleworker Satisfaction with Telework Programs?," *Review of Public Personnel Administration* 40, no. 1 (March 2020): 36–55.

7. Prithwiraj Choudhury, Jacqueline N. Lane, and Iavor Bojinov, "Virtual Water Coolers: A Field Experiment on the Role of Virtual Interactions on Organizational Newcomer Performance," working paper 21-125, Harvard Business School, Boston, 2023.

8. Geoff Colvin, "Get Back to Work!," *Fortune* 185, no. 2 (May 4, 2022): 88–94.

9. Lisa Rein, "Patent Office Workers Bilked the Government of Millions by Playing Hooky, Watchdog Finds," *The Washington Post*, August 31, 2016, https://www.washingtonpost.com/news/powerpost/wp/2016/08/31/patent-office-workers-cost-taxpayers-millions-by-playing-hooky-watchdog-finds/.

10. For examples, see Cooper and Kurland, "Telecommuting, Professional Isolation, and Employee Development in Public and Private Organizations"; Golden, Veiga, and Dino, "The Impact of Professional Isolation on Teleworker Job Performance"; Tammy D. Allen, Timothy D. Golden, and Kristen M. Shockley, "How Effective Is Telecommuting? Assessing the Status of Our Scientific Findings," *Psychological Science in the Public Interest* 16, no. 2 (October 2015): 40–68.

11. Catherine Durnell Cramton, Kara L. Orvis, and Jeanne M. Wilson, "Situation Invisibility and Attribution in Distributed Collaborations," *Journal of Management* 33, no. 4 (August 1, 2007): 525–546.

12. Colvin, "Get Back to Work!"

13. Interview with a WFA technical worker, November 2019.

14. Lucy Meakin, "Remote Working's Longer Hours Are New Normal for Many," *Bloomberg*, February 2, 2021, https://www.bloomberg.com/news/articles/2021-02-02/remote-working-s-longer-hours-are-new-normal-for-many-chart.

15. Justin Anker and Patrick R. Krill, "Stress, Drink, Leave: An Examination of Gender-Specific Risk Factors for Mental Health Problems and Attrition among Licensed Attorneys," *PloS One* 16, no. 5 (2021): e0250563, https://doi.org/10.1371/journal.pone.0250563.

16. "Goldman Sachs Raises Banker Pay after 95-Hour Week Complaint," *BBC News*, August 2, 2021, https://www.bbc.com/news/business-58054983.

17. Anne-Laure Fayard and John Weeks, "Photocopiers and Water-Coolers: The Affordances of Informal Interaction," *Organization Studies* 28, no. 5 (May 1, 2007): 605–634, https://doi.org/10.1177/0170840606068310.

18. Paul Levy, "Companies Are Trying to Connect Remote Workers with 'Virtual Water Coolers'—but It's Harder Than It Sounds," The Conversation, September 23, 2020, http://theconversation.com/companies-are-trying-to-connect-remote-workers-with-virtual-water-coolers-but-its-harder-than-it-sounds-146505.

19. Pamela J. Hinds and Mark Mortensen, "Understanding Conflict in Geographically Distributed Teams: The Moderating Effects of Shared Identity, Shared Context, and Spontaneous Communication," *Organization Science* 16, no. 3 (2005): 290–307.

20. Choudhury, Lane, and Bojinov, "Virtual Water Coolers."

21. Cristobal Young and Chaeyoon Lim, "Time as a Network Good: Evidence from Unemployment and the Standard Workweek," *Sociological Science* 1 (2014): 10–27, https://doi.org/10.15195/v1.a2.

22. Wade Foster, "How to Run a Company Retreat for a Remote Team," Zapier, April 1, 2019, https://zapier.com/blog/how-run-company-retreat-remote-team/.

23. Foster, "How to Run a Company Retreat."

24. Sen Chai and Richard B. Freeman, "Temporary Colocation and Collaborative Discovery: Who Confers at Conferences," *Strategic Management Journal* 40, no. 13 (2019): 2138–2164, https://doi.org/10.1002/smj.3062; Kevin J. Boudreau et al., "A Field Experiment on Search Costs and the Formation of Scientific Collaborations," *The Review of Economics and Statistics* 99, no. 4 (October 2017): 565–576, https://doi.org/10.1162/REST_a_00676.

25. Prithwiraj Choudhury, "Innovation Outcomes in a Distributed Organization: Intrafirm Mobility and Access to Resources," *Organization Science* 28, no. 2 (April 2017): 339–354, https://doi.org/10.1287/orsc.2017.1121; Caroline Viola Fry, "Bridging the Gap: Evidence from the Return Migration of African Scientists," *Organization Science* 34, no. 1 (2023): 404–432, https://doi.org/10.1287/orsc.2022.1580;

Christos Kolympiris, Sebastian Hoenen, and Peter G. Klein, "Learning by Seconding: Evidence from National Science Foundation Rotators," *Organization Science* 30, no. 3 (April 19, 2019): 528–551.

26. Nune Hovhannisyan and Wolfgang Keller, "International Business Travel: An Engine of Innovation?," *Journal of Economic Growth* 20, no. 1 (March 1, 2015): 75–104, https://doi.org/10.1007/s10887-014-9107-7; Michele Coscia, Frank M. H. Neffke, and Ricardo Hausmann, "Knowledge Diffusion in the Network of International Business Travel," *Nature Human Behaviour* 4, no. 10 (October 2020): 1011–1020, https://doi.org/10.1038/s41562-020-0922-x.

27. Dany Bahar et al., "Innovation on Wings: Nonstop Flights and Firm Innovation in the Global Context," *Management Science* 69, no. 10 (March 3, 2023): 6202–6223, https://doi.org/10.1287/mnsc.2023.4682.

28. For example, Terry L. Besser, *Team Toyota: Transplanting the Toyota Culture to the Camry Plant in Kentucky*, SUNY Series in the Sociology of Work (Albany: State University of New York Press, 1996); Anders Edström and Jay R. Galbraith, "Transfer of Managers as a Coordination and Control Strategy in Multinational Organizations," *Administrative Science Quarterly* 22, no. 2 (1977): 248–263, https://doi.org/10.2307/2391959.

29. Victoria Sevcenko et al., "Office at Offsite: How Temporary Colocation Shapes Communication in an All-Remote Organization," INSEAD working paper no. 2024/39/STR/OBH, May 11, 2024, http://dx.doi.org/10.2139/ssrn.4825368.

30. Patricia Simões Aelbrecht, "'Fourth Places': The Contemporary Public Settings for Informal Social Interaction among Strangers," *Journal of Urban Design* 21, no. 1 (2016): 124–152, https://doi.org/10.1080/13574809.2015.1106920.

31. Prithwiraj Choudhury, Ruth Costas, and Pedro Levindo, "The Future of Start-Up Chile," Case 622-080 (Harvard Business School, Boston, 2021).

32. Choudhury, Costas, and Levindo, "The Future of Start-Up Chile."

33. Amir Salihefendic (@amix3k), "Next week, we are having a Doist company retreat in Ireland. . . . ," Twitter (now X), September 19, 2024, https://x.com/amix3k/status/1836812704679424248.

34. Boudreau et al., "A Field Experiment on Search Costs"; Sari Pekkala Kerr and William R. Kerr, "Global Collaborative Patents," *The Economic Journal* 128, no. 612 (2018): F235–272, https://doi.org/10.1111/ecoj.12369.

35. Miller McPherson, Lynn Smith-Lovin, and James M. Cook, "Birds of a Feather: Homophily in Social Networks," *Annual Review of Sociology* 27, no. 1 (2001): 415-444.

Chapter 6

1. Jose Maria Barrero, Nicholas Bloom, and Steven J. Davis, "Why Working from Home Will Stick," working paper 28731, National Bureau of Economic Research, April 2021, https://www.nber.org/papers/w28731.

2. Barrero, Bloom, and Davis, "Why Working from Home Will Stick."

3. Sarah Green Carmichael, "Actually, Zoom's In-Office Policy Shows the Power of Hybrid Work," *The Washington Post,* August 8, 2023, https://www.washingtonpost.com/business/2023/08/08/actually-zoom-s-in-office-policy-shows-the-power-of-hybrid-work/7453bef0-35fe-11ee-ac4e-e707870e43db_story.html.

4. Peter Eavis, Julie Creswell, and Joe Rennison, "Why Office Buildings Are Still in Trouble," *The New York Times,* November 17, 2022, https://www.nytimes.com/2022/11/17/business/office-buildings-real-estate-vacancy.html.

5. Matthew Boyle, "Hybrid Work Patterns Suggest Thursday Is the New Monday," *Los Angeles Times,* December 22, 2022, https://www.latimes.com/business/story/2022-12-22/thursday-new-monday-hybrid-work-patterns-shift.

6. "Why Is JR East's Private Office 'STATION BOOTH' So Successful?," Impress Watch, accessed September 13, 2023, https://www.watch.impress.co.jp/docs/topic/1436187.html.

7. Kevin Truong, "This SF Startup Wants to Be the Airbnb of Commercial Real Estate," *The San Francisco Standard,* December 21, 2022, https://sfstandard.com/2022/12/21/this-sf-startup-wants-to-be-the-airbnb-of-commercial-real-estate/.

8. "Radious Is a Non-Traditional Solution for a Remote Workforce," Radious, https://hello.radious.pro/work-revolution.

9. N. Sharon Hill et al., "Building Employee Commitment to Change across Organizational Levels: The Influence of Hierarchical Distance and Direct Managers' Transformational Leadership," *Organization Science* 23, no. 3 (June 2012): 758–777, https://doi.org/10.1287/orsc.1110.0662.

Epilogue

1. Jose Maria Barrero, Nicholas Bloom, and Steven J. Davis, "Why Working from Home Will Stick," working paper 28731, National Bureau of Economic Research, April 2021, https://www.nber.org/papers/w28731.

Appendix B

1. Edward L. Glaeser, "Introduction to 'Agglomeration Economics,'" in *Agglomeration Economics* (Chicago: University of Chicago Press, 2010), 1–14.

2. Richard Florida, "Cities and the Creative Class," *City & Community* 2, no. 1 (2003): 3–19; Edward Glaeser, *Triumph of the City: How Our Greatest Invention Makes Us Richer, Smarter, Greener, Healthier, and Happier* (New York: Penguin Publishing Group, 2011).

3. Margherita Balconi, Stefano Breschi, and Francesco Lissoni, "Networks of Inventors and the Role of Academia: An Exploration of Italian Patent Data," *Research Policy* 33, no. 1 (January 2004): 127–145, https://doi.org/10.1016/S0048-7333(03)00108-2.

4. A. B. Jaffe, M. Trajtenberg, and R. Henderson, "Geographic Localization of Knowledge Spillovers as Evidenced by Patent Citations," *Quarterly Journal of Economics* 108, no. 3 (1993): 577–598; P. Almeida and B. Kogut, "Localization of Knowledge and the Mobility of Engineers in Regional Networks," *Management Science* 45, no. 7 (July 1999): 905–917, https://doi.org/10.1287/mnsc.45.7.905.

5. A. Agrawal, D. Kapur, and J. McHale, "How Do Spatial and Social Proximity Influence Knowledge Flows? Evidence from Patent Data," *Journal of Urban Economics* 64, no. 2 (2008): 258–269; J. Singh, "Collaborative Networks as Determinants of Knowledge Diffusion Patterns," *Management Science* 51, no. 5 (2005): 756–770.

6. S. Breschi and F. Lissoni, "Mobility of Skilled Workers and Co-Invention Networks: An Anatomy of Localized Knowledge Flows," *Journal of Economic Geography* 9, no. 4 (2009): 439–468.

7. Agrawal, Kapur, and McHale, "How Do Spatial and Social Proximity Influence Knowledge Flows?"; Singh, "Collaborative Networks"; P. Almeida, A. Phene, and S. Li, "The Influence of Ethnic Community Knowledge on Indian Inventor Innovativeness," *Organization Science* 26, no. 1 (2014): 198–217.

8. Prithwiraj Choudhury, and Do Yoon Kim, "The Ethnic Migrant Inventor Effect: Codification and Recombination of Knowledge across Borders," *Strategic Management Journal* 40, no. 2 (2019): 203–229.

9. Choudhury and Kim, "The Ethnic Migrant Inventor Effect."

10. S. H. Baruffaldi and P. Landoni, "Return Mobility and Scientific Productivity of Researchers Working Abroad: The Role of Home Country Linkages," *Research Policy* 41, no. 9 (2012): 1655–1665; K. Jonkers and L. Cruz-Castro, "Research upon Return: The Effect of International Mobility on Scientific Ties, Production and Impact," *Research Policy* 42,

no. 8 (2013): 1366–1377; G. Scellato, C. Franzoni, and P. Stephan, "Migrant Scientists and International Networks," *Research Policy* 44, no. 1 (2015): 108–120.

11. E. Ferrucci and F. Lissoni, "Foreign Inventors in Europe and the United States: Diversity and Patent Quality," *Research Policy* 48, no. 9 (2019): 103774; R. B. Freeman and W. Huang, "Collaborating with People Like Me: Ethnic Coauthorship within the United States," *Journal of Labor Economics* 33, no. S1 (2015): S289–S318; S. P. Kerr, and W. R. Kerr, "Global Collaborative Patents," *Economic Journal* 128, no. 612 (2018): F235–F272.

12. M. A. Carpenter, W. G. Sanders, and H. B. Gregersen, "Bundling Human Capital with Organizational Context: The Impact of International Assignment Experience on Multinational Firm Performance and CEO Pay," *Academy of Management Journal* 44, no. 3 (2017): 493–511; S. R. Fitzsimmons, "Multicultural Employees: A Framework for Understanding How They Contribute to Organizations," *Academy of Management Review* 38, no. 4 (2013): 525–549; F. C. Godart et al., "Fashion with a Foreign Flair: Professional Experiences Abroad Facilitate the Creative Innovations of Organizations," *Academy of Management Journal* 58, no. 1 (2015): 195–220; M. R. Haas, "Acquiring and Applying Knowledge in Transnational Teams: The Roles of Cosmopolitans and Locals," *Organization Science* 17, no. 3 (2006): 367–384; S. Jang, "Cultural Brokerage and Creative Performance in Multicultural Teams," *Organization Science* 28, no. 6 (2017): 993–1009; S. Le and M. Kroll, "CEO International Experience: Effects on Strategic Change and Firm Performance," *Journal of International Business Studies* 48, no. 4 (2017): 573–595; E. Seo, H. Kang, and J. Song, "Blending Talents for Innovation: Team Composition for Crossborder R&D Collaboration within Multinational Corporations," *Journal of International Business Studies* 51, no. 5 (2020): 851–885.

13. C. M. Daily, S. T. Certo, and D. R. Dalton, "International Experience in the Executive Suite: The Path to Prosperity?," *Strategic Management Journal* 21, no. 4 (2000): 515–523; Carpenter, Sanders, and Gregersen, "Bundling Human Capital"; Godart et al., "Fashion with a Foreign Flair"; Jang, "Cultural Brokerage"; Le and Kroll, "CEO International Experience."

14. AnnaLee Saxenian, *The New Argonauts: Regional Advantage in a Global Economy* (Cambridge, MA: Harvard University Press, 2006).

15. G. J. Borjas and K. B. Doran, "The Collapse of the Soviet Union and the Productivity of American Mathematicians," *Quarterly Journal of Economics* 127, no. 3 (2012): 1143–1203; E. Ferrucci, "Migration, Innovation and Technological Diversion: German Patenting after the Collapse of the Soviet Union," *Research Policy* 49, no. 9 (2020): 104057,

doi: 10.1016/j.respol.2020.104057; I. Ganguli, "Immigration and Ideas: What Did Russian Scientists 'Bring' to the United States?," *Journal of Labor Economics* 33, no. 51 (S1) (2015): S257–S288; P. Moser, A. Voena, and F. Waldinger, "German Jewish Émigrés and U.S. Invention," *American Economic Review* 104, no. 10 (2014): 3222–3255; E. Hornung, "Immigration and the Diffusion of Technology: The Huguenot Diaspora in Prussia," *American Economic Review* 104, no. 1 (2014): 84–122.

16. Freeman and Huang, "Collaborating with People Like Me"; Kerr and Kerr, "Global Collaborative Patents"; Carpenter, Sanders, and Gregersen, "Bundling Human Capital"; Fitzsimmons, "Multicultural Employees"; Seo, Kang, and Song, "Blending Talents for Innovation"; Jang, "Cultural Brokerage"; J. Hunt and M. Gauthier-Loiselle, "How Much Does Immigration Boost Innovation?," *American Economic Journal: Macroeconomics* 2, no. 2 (2010): 31–56; S. Breschi, F. Lissoni, and E. Miguélez, "Foreign-Origin Inventors in the USA: Testing for Diaspora and Brain Gain Effects," *Journal of Economic Geography* 17, no. 5 (2017): 1009–1038; J. Edler, H. Fier, and C. Grimpe, "International Scientist Mobility and the Locus of Knowledge and Technology Transfer," *Research Policy* 40, no. 6 (2011): 791–805; T. A. Fackler, Y. Giesing, and N. Laurentsyeva, "Knowledge Remittances: Does Emigration Foster Innovation?," *Research Policy* 49, no. 9 (2020): 103863, doi: 10.1016/j.respol.2019.103863; J. Gibson and D. McKenzie, "Scientific Mobility and Knowledge Networks in High Emigration Countries: Evidence from the Pacific," *Research Policy* 43, no. 9 (2014): 1486–1495.

17. Prithwiraj Choudhury, "Return Migration and Geography of Innovation in MNEs: A Natural Experiment of Knowledge Production by Local Workers Reporting to Return Migrants," *Journal of Economic Geography* 16, no. 3 (2016): 585–610.

18. D. Bahar, P. Choudhury, and H. Rapoport, "Migrant Inventors and the Technological Advantage of Nations," *Research Policy* 49, no. 9 (2020): 103947, doi: 10.1016/j.respol.2020.103947.

19. J. Blit, M. Skuterud, and J. Zhang, "Can Skilled Immigration Raise Innovation? Evidence from Canadian Cities," *Journal of Economic Geography* 20, no. 4 (2020): 879–901; D. Crown, A. Faggian, and J. Corcoran, "Foreign-Born Graduates and Innovation: Evidence from an Australian Skilled Visa Program," *Research Policy* 49, no. 9 (2020): 103945, doi:10.1016/j.respol.2020.103945.

20. A. Agrawal, I. Cockburn, and J. McHale, "Gone but Not Forgotten: Knowledge Flows, Labor Mobility, and Enduring Social Relationships," *Journal of Economic Geography* 6, no. 5 (2006): 571–591; C. V. Fry, "Building Bridges: The Impact of Return Migration by African Scientists," 2020 Doctoral Research Forum and Thesis Prize (Cambridge, MA: MIT

Sloan School of Management, 2020), https://www.youtube.com/watch?v=Jf-lxojyDqM; A. Oettl and A. Agrawal, "International Labor Mobility and Knowledge Flow Externalities," *Journal of International Business Studies* 39 (2008): 1242–1260; R. Madhavan and A. Iriyama, "Understanding Global Flows of Venture Capital: Human Networks as the 'Carrier Wave' of Globalization," *Journal of International Business Studies* 40, no. 8 (2009): 1241–1259.

21. G. Dokko and L. Rosenkopf, "Social Capital for Hire? Mobility of Technical Professionals and Firm Influence in Wireless Standards Committees," *Organization Science* 21, no. 3 (2009): 677–695.

22. A. Kalnins and W. Chung, "Social Capital, Geography, and Survival: Gujarati Immigrant Entrepreneurs in the U.S. Lodging Industry," *Management Science* 52, no. 2 (2006): 233–247; Elena Kulchina and Exequiel Hernandez, "Immigrants and Firm Performance: Effects on Foreign Subsidiaries versus Foreign Entrepreneurs," in *Academy of Management Proceedings*, vol. 2016, no. 1 (Briarcliff Manor, NY: Academy of Management, 2016), 10833; Horatio M. Morgan, Sui Sui, and Shavin Malhotra, "The Effect of Exporting to Country of Origin on the Financial Performance of Immigrant-Owned SMEs," in *Academy of Management Proceedings,* vol. 2020, no. 1 (Briarcliff Manor, NY: Academy of Management, 2020), 10060; M. Kenney, D. Breznitz, and M. Murphree, "Coming Back Home after the Sun Rises: Returnee Entrepreneurs and Growth of High Tech Industries," *Research Policy* 42, no. 2 (2013): 391–407; E. Kulchina, "Personal Preferences, Entrepreneurs' Location Choices, and Firm Performance," *Management Science* 62, no. 6 (2015): 1814–1829; Godart et al., "Fashion with a Foreign Flair"; A. Banerjee and K. Munshi, "How Efficiently Is Capital Allocated? Evidence from the Knitted Garment Industry in Tirupur," *Review of Economic Studies* 71, no. 1 (2004): 19–42; J. Canello, "Migrant Entrepreneurs and Local Networks in Industrial Districts," *Research Policy* 45, no. 10 (2016): 1953–1964; S. P. Kerr and W. R. Kerr, "Immigrant Entrepreneurship in America: Evidence from the Survey of Business Owners 2007 & 2012," *Research Policy* 49, no. 3 (2020): 103918, doi: 10.1016/j.respol.2019.103918; E. Kulchina, "A Path to Value Creation for Foreign Entrepreneurs," *Strategic Management Journal* 37, no. 7 (2016): 1240–1262.

23. Kerr and Kerr, "Immigrant Entrepreneurship in America."

24. J. Wahba and Y. Zenou, "Out of Sight, Out of Mind: Migration, Entrepreneurship and Social Capital," *Regional Science and Urban Economics* 42, no. 5 (2012): 890–903.

25. M. G. Herander and L. A. Saavedra, "Exports and the Structure of Immigrant-Based Networks: The Role of Geographic Proximity," *Review of Economics and Statistics* 87, no. 2 (2005): 323–335.

26. P. M. Vaaler, "Immigrant Remittances and the Venture Investment Environment of Developing Countries," *Journal of International Business Studies* 42 (2011): 1121–1149.

27. A. Edström and J. Galbraith, "Transfer of Managers as a Coordination and Control Strategy in Multinational Organizations," *Administrative Science Quarterly* 22, no. 2 (1977): 248–263; T. L. Madsen, E. Mosakowski, and S. Zaheer, "Knowledge Retention and Personnel Mobility: The Nondisruptive Effects of Inflows of Experience," *Organization Science* 14, no. 2 (2003): 173–191.

28. Choudhury, "Return Migration and Geography of Innovation"; Prithwiraj Choudhury, "Innovation Outcomes in a Distributed Organization: Intra-Firm Mobility and Access to Resources," *Organization Science* 28, no. 2 (2017): 339–354; Edström and Galbraith, "Transfer of Managers as a Coordination and Control Strategy."

29. Y.-C. Chen, "The Limits of Brain Circulation: Chinese Returnees and Technological Development in Beijing," *Pacific Affairs* 81, no. 2 (2008): 195–215; J. Luo, D. Chen, and J. Chen, "Coming Back and Giving Back: Returnee Directors and Corporate Donations," *Academy of Management Proceedings*, 2016, doi:10.5465/ambpp.2016.215; Saxenian, *The New Argonauts.*

30. Le and Kroll, "CEO International Experience"; Saxenian, *The New Argonauts*; J. Singh and A. Agrawal, "Recruiting for Ideas: How Firms Exploit the Prior Inventions of New Hires," *Management Science* 57, no. 1 (2010): 129–150; J. Song, P. Almeida, and G. Wu, "Learning-by-Hiring: When Is Mobility More Likely to Facilitate Interfirm Knowledge Transfer?," *Management Science* 49, no. 4 (2003): 351–365.

31. Choudhury and Kim, "The Ethnic Migrant Inventor Effect"; Saxenian, *The New Argonauts*; S. P. Kerr et al., "Global Talent Flows," *Journal of Economic Perspectives* 30, no. 4 (2016): 83–106.

32. S. Chattopadhyay and P. Choudhury, "Sink or Swim: The Role of Workplace Context in Shaping Career Advancement and Human-Capital Development," *Organization Science* 28, no. 2 (2017): 211–227.

33. M. A. Clemens, "Why Do Programmers Earn More in Houston Than Hyderabad? Evidence from Randomized Processing of U.S. Visas," *American Economic Review* 103, no. 3 (2013): 198–202; L. Hendricks and T. Schoellman, "Human Capital and Development Accounting: New Evidence from Wage Gains at Migration," *Quarterly Journal of Economics* 133, no. 2 (2018): 665–700; Enrico Moretti, *The New Geography of Jobs* (Boston: Houghton Mifflin Harcourt, 2012); P.-A. Edin, P. Fredriksson, and O. Åslund, "Ethnic Enclaves and the Economic Success of Immigrants—Evidence from a Natural Experiment," *Quarterly Journal of*

Economics 118, no. 1 (2003): 329–357; E. L. Glaeser and D. C. Maré, "Cities and Skills," *Journal of Labor Economics* 19, no. 2 (2001): 316–342.

34. J. Hunt, "Which Immigrants Are Most Innovative and Entrepreneurial? Distinctions by Entry Visa," *Journal of Labor Economics* 29, no. 3 (2011): 417–457.

35. Fry, "Building Bridges"; Choudhury, "Innovation Outcomes in a Distributed Organization"; Prithwiraj Choudhury, "Intra-Firm Geographic Mobility: Value Creation Mechanisms and Future Research Directions," in *Employee Inter- and Intra-Firm Mobility,* ed. D. Tzabbar and B. Cirillo (Bingley, UK: Emerald, 2020), 179–195.

36. Kulchina, "A Path to Value Creation."

37. As discussed in greater detail in Prithwiraj Choudhury, "Geographic Mobility, Immobility, and Geographic Flexibility: A Review and Agenda for Research on the Changing Geography of Work," *Academy of Management Annals* 16, no. 1 (2022): 258–296.

38. Michael A. Clemens, "Economics and Emigration: Trillion-Dollar Bills on the Sidewalk?," *Journal of Economic Perspectives* 25, no. 3 (August 2011): 83–106; Yang Song, "What Should Economists Know about the Current Chinese Hukou System?," *China Economic Review* 29 (June 2014): 200–212; U. Akcigit, S. Baslandze, and S. Stantcheva, "Taxation and the International Mobility of Inventors," *American Economic Review* 106, no. 10 (2016): 2930–2981; E. Moretti and D. J. Wilson, "The Effect of State Taxes on the Geographical Location of Top Earners: Evidence from Star Scientists," *American Economic Review* 107, no. 7 (2017): 1858–1903; D. Schleicher, "Stuck! The Law and Economics of Residential Stagnation," *Yale Law Journal* 127, no. 1 (2017): 78–154; T. J. Cooke, C. H. Mulder, and M. Thomas, "Union Dissolution and Migration," *Demographic Research* 34, article 26 (2016): 741–759.

39. K. W. Chan, "China's Hukou Reform Remains a Major Challenge to Domestic Migrants in Cities," World Bank, December 17, 2021, https://blogs.worldbank.org/peoplemove/chinas-hukou-reform-remains-major-challenge-domestic-migrants-cities; Song, "What Should Economists Know about the Current Chinese Hukou System?"

40. X. Wu and D. J. Treiman, "Inequality and Equality under Chinese Socialism: The Hukou System and Intergenerational Occupational Mobility," *American Journal of Sociology* 113, no. 2 (2007): 415–445; Chan, "China's Hukou Reform."

41. Wu and Treiman, "Inequality and Equality."

42. B. A. Rissing and E. J. Castilla, "Testing Attestations: U.S. Unemployment and Immigrant Work Authorizations," *Industrial & Labor Relations Review* 69, no. 5 (2016): 1081–1113; S. Orazbayev, "International

Knowledge Flows and the Administrative Barriers to Mobility," *Research Policy* 46, no. 9 (2017): 1655–1665; S. Kahn and M. MacGarvie, "The Impact of Permanent Residency Delays for STEM PhDs: Who Leaves and Why," *Research Policy* 49, no. 9 (2020): 103879, doi: 10.1016/j.respol.2019.103879; T. Kato and C. Sparber, "Quotas and Quality: The Effect of H-1B Visa Restrictions on the Pool of Prospective Undergraduate Students from Abroad," *Review of Economics and Statistics* 95, no. 1 (2013): 109–126.

43. S. Kahn and M. MacGarvie, "Do Return Requirements Increase International Knowledge Diffusion? Evidence from the Fulbright Program," *Research Policy* 45, no. 6 (2016): 1304–1322.

44. B. Austin, E. Glaeser, and L. H. Summers, "Saving the Heartland: Place-Based Policies in 21st Century America," in *Brookings Papers on Economic Activity*, ed. J. Eberly and J. Stock (Spring 2018): 151–255; P. Choudhury et al., "Food Security and Human Mobility during the Covid-19 Lockdown," working paper 20-113, Harvard Business School, Boston, 2020; Z. L. Kone et al., "Internal Borders and Migration in India," *Journal of Economic Geography* 18, no. 4 (2018): 729–759.

45. G. Scheffler and R. Nunn, "Occupational Licensing and the Limits of Public Choice Theory," All Faculty Scholarship at Penn Law, 2072 (2019), https://scholarship.law.upenn.edu/faculty_scholarship/2072.

46. B. D. Peterson, S. S. Pandya, and D. Leblang, "Doctors with Borders: Occupational Licensing as an Implicit Barrier to High Skill Migration," *Public Choice* 160, nos. 1–2 (2014): 45–63.

47. Moretti and Wilson, "The Effect of State Taxes"; J. Johnson and M. Kleiner, "Is Occupational Licensing a Barrier to Interstate Migration?," *American Economic Journal: Economic Policy* 12, no. 3 (2020): 347–373; Choudhury et al., "Food Security and Human Mobility"; Kone et al., "Internal Borders and Migration in India"; Scheffler and Nunn, "Occupational Licensing."

48. T. W. Lee, T. C. Burch, and T. R. Mitchell, "The Story of Why We Stay: A Review of Job Embeddedness," *Annual Review of Organizational Psychology and Organizational Behavior* 1 (2014): 199–216.

49. R. M. Costrell and M. Podgursky, "Distribution of Benefits in Teacher Retirement Systems and Their Implications for Mobility," *Education Finance and Policy* 5, no. 4 (2010): 519–557; T. C. Buchmueller and R. G. Valletta, "The Effects of Employer-Provided Health Insurance on Worker Mobility," *Industrial & Labor Relations Review* 49, no. 3 (1996): 439–455.

50. E. Starr, M. Ganco, and B. A. Campbell, "Strategic Human Capital Management in the Context of Cross-Industry and Within-Industry Mobility Frictions," *Strategic Management Journal* 39, no. 8 (2018):

2226–2254; M. Marx, D. Strumsky, and L. Fleming, "Mobility, Skills, and the Michigan Non-Compete Experiment," *Management Science* 55, no. 6 (2009): 875–889.

51. S. Bowles, "Migration as Investment: Empirical Tests of the Human Investment Approach to Geographical Mobility," *Review of Economics and Statistics* 52, no. 4 (1970): 356–362; M. J. Greenwood, "Research on Internal Migration in the United States: A Survey," *Journal of Economic Literature* 13, no. 2 (1975): 397–433; P. N. Ritchey, "Explanations of Migration," *Annual Review of Sociology* 2 (1976): 363–404; K. Munshi and M. Rosenzweig, "Why Is Mobility in India So Low? Social Insurance, Inequality, and Growth," working paper 14850, National Bureau of Economic Research, Cambridge, MA, 2009, https://www.nber.org/system/files/working_papers/w14850/w14850.pdf.

52. Song, "What Should Economists Know?"; K. Munshi and M. Rosenzweig, "Networks and Misallocation: Insurance, Migration, and the Rural-Urban Wage Gap," *American Economic Review* 106, no. 1 (2016): 46–98.

53. K. Chen, S. Chiang, and S. F. Leung, "Migration, Family, and Risk Diversification," *Journal of Labor Economics* 21, no. 21 (2003): 353–380.

54. M. L. Blackburn, "Internal Migration and the Earnings of Married Couples in the United States," *Journal of Economic Geography* 10, no. 1 (2010): 87–111; D. A. Widiss, "Reconfiguring Sex, Gender, and the Law of Marriage," *Family Court Review* 50, no. 2 (2012): 205–213; O. Sorenson and M. S. Dahl, "Geography, Joint Choices, and the Reproduction of Gender Inequality," *American Sociological Review* 81, no. 5 (2016): 900–920; N. Schoenbaum, "Stuck or Rooted: The Costs of Mobility and the Value of Place," *Yale Law Journal Forum* 127 (2017): 458–479; S. H. Sandell, "Women and the Economics of Family Migration," *Review of Economics and Statistics* 59, no. 4 (1977): 406–414; J. Mincer, "Family Migration Decisions," *Journal of Political Economy* 86, no. 5 (1978): 749–773; Lee, Burch, and Mitchell, "The Story of Why We Stay."

55. A. Speare, F. Kobrin, and W. Kingkade, "The Influence of Socioeconomic Bonds and Satisfaction on Interstate Migration," *Social Forces* 61, no. 2 (1982): 551–574.

56. S. E. Yonker, "Geography and the Market for CEOs," *Management Science* 63, no. 3 (2016): 609–630; E. Kulchina, "Personal Preferences, Entrepreneurs' Location Choices, and Firm Performance," *Management Science* 62, no. 6 (2015): 1814–1829; M. S. Dahl and O. Sorenson, "The Migration of Technical Workers," *Journal of Urban Economics* 67, no. 1 (2010): 33–45; S. Bertoli and I. Ruyssen, "Networks and Migrants' Intended Destination," *Journal of Economic Geography* 18, no. 4 (2018):

705–728; Q. David, A. Janiak, and E. Wasmer, "Local Social Capital and Geographical Mobility," *Journal of Urban Economics* 68, no. 2 (2010): 191–204.

57. Schoenbaum, "Stuck or Rooted"; D. Schleicher, "Surreply: How and Why We Should Become Un-*Stuck!*," *Yale Law Journal Forum* 127 (2017): 571–588.

58. P. Choudhury, S. Dutta, and O. Kwon, "Geographic Mobility and Punctuated Renewal of Social Attachment," working paper 19-010, Harvard Business School, Boston, 2021.

59. P. Choudhury, "Geographic Mobility, Immobility, and Geographic Flexibility: A Review and Agenda for Research on the Changing Geography of Work," *Academy of Management Annals* 16, no. 1 (2022): 258–296.

60. G. Hofstede, *Culture's Consequences: International Differences in Work-Related Values* (Beverly Hills, CA: SAGE, 1980); H. Berry, M. F. Guillén, and N. Zhou, "An Institutional Approach to Cross-National Distance," *Journal of International Business Studies* 41 (2010): 1460–1480.

61. J. S. Black and M. E. Mendenhall, "The U-Curve Adjustment Hypothesis Revisited: A Review and Theoretical Framework," *Journal of International Business Studies* 22 (1991): 225–247; G. K. Stahl et al., "The Upside of Cultural Differences," *Cross Cultural & Strategic Management* 24, no. 1 (2017): 2–12; M. Lazarova, M. Westman, and M. A. Shaffer, "Elucidating the Positive Side of the Work–Family Interface on International Assignments: A Model of Expatriate Work and Family Performance," *Academy of Management Review* 35, no. 1 (2010): 93–117.

62. Robert Kanigel, *The Man Who Knew Infinity* (New York: Simon and Schuster, 2013).

63. Sunil S. Amrith, *Migration and Diaspora in Modern Asia,* vol. 7 (New York: Cambridge University Press, 2011).

64. Bowles, "Migration as Investment"; G. M. Dahl, "Mobility and the Return of Education: Testing a Roy Model with Multiple Markets," *Econometrica* 70, no. 6 (2002): 2367–2420; E. L. Glaeser and D. C. Maré, "Cities and Skills," *Journal of Labor Economics* 19, no. 2 (2001): 316–342; J. Grogger and G. H. Hanson, "Attracting Talent: Location Choices of Foreign-Born PhDs in the United States," *Journal of Labor Economics* 33, no. S1 (2015): S5–S38; Joint Economic Committee, "Losing Our Minds: Brain Drain across the United States," SCP report no. 2-19, Social Capital Project, Washington, DC, 2019.

65. Greenwood, "Research on International Migration."

66. S. Raphael and D. A. Riker, "Geographic Mobility, Race, and Wage Differentials," *Journal of Urban Economics* 45, no. 1 (1999): 17–46; B. Schmutz and M. Sidibé, "Frictional Labour Mobility," *Review of Economic Studies* 86, no. 4 (2019): 1779–1826; Mincer, "Family Migration Decisions."

67. S. R. Foster, "The Limits of Mobility and the Persistence of Urban Inequality," *Yale Law Journal Forum* 127 (2017): 480–497; P. Ganong and D. Shoag, "Why Has Regional Income Convergence in the U.S. Declined?," *Journal of Urban Economics* 102 (2017): 76–90; D. F. Heuermann and J. F. Schmieder, "The Effect of Infrastructure on Worker Mobility: Evidence from High-Speed Rail Expansion in Germany," *Journal of Economic Geography* 19, no. 2 (2019): 335–372; Austin, Glaeser, and Summers, "Saving the Heartland"; E. L. Glaeser et al., "The Rise of the Skilled City [with comments]," in *Brookings-Wharton Papers on Urban Affairs*, ed. W. G. Gale and J. Rothenberg Pack (Washington, DC: Brookings Institution Press, 2004), 47–105.

68. Ritchey, "Explanations of Migration"; A. Head and H. Lloyd-Ellis, "Housing Liquidity, Mobility, and the Labour Market," *Review of Economic Studies* 79, no. 4 (2012): 1559–1589.

69. Bowles, "Migration as Investment"; Greenwood, "Research on Internal Migration"; Schmutz and Sidibé, "Frictional Labour Mobility."

70. A. Agrawal, A. Galasso, and A. Oettl, "Roads and Innovation," *Review of Economics and Statistics* 99, no. 3 (2017): 417–434; R. Jensen, "Do Labor Market Opportunities Affect Young Women's Work and Family Decisions? Experimental Evidence from India," *Quarterly Journal of Economics* 127, no. 2 (2012): 753–792; M. J. Greenwood, "An Analysis of the Determinants of Geographic Labor Mobility in the United States," *Review of Economics and Statistics* 51, no. 2 (1969): 189–194.

71. "Managing International Migration under Covid-19," policy paper, Organisation for Economic Co-operation and Development, Paris, 2020; A. Mesnard and P. Seabright, "Escaping Epidemics through Migration? Quarantine Measures under Incomplete Information about Infection Risk," *Journal of Public Economics* 93, nos. 7–8 (2009): 931–938.

72. C. Farbotko and H. Lazrus, "The First Climate Refugees? Contesting Global Narratives of Climate Change in Tuvalu," *Global Environmental Change* 22, no. 2 (2012): 382–390; R. Black et al., "Migration, Immobility and Displacement Outcomes following Extreme Events," *Environmental Science & Policy* 27, Suppl. 1 (2013): S32–S43; F. Biermann and I. Boas, "Preparing for a Warmer World: Towards a Global Governance System to Protect Climate Refugees," *Global Environmental Politics* 10, no. 1 (2010): 60–88; B. Entwisle, A. Verdery, and N. Williams, "Climate Change and Migration: New Insights from a Dynamic Model of Out-Migration and Return Migration," *American Journal of Sociology* 125, no. 6 (2020): 1469–1512.

73. Jose Maria Barrero, Nicholas Bloom, and Steven J. Davis, "Why Working from Home Will Stick," working paper 28731, National Bureau of Economic Research, April 2021, https://www.nber.org/papers/w28731.

74. Prithwiraj Choudhury et al., "Is Hybrid Work the Best of Both Worlds? Evidence from a Field Experiment," *Review of Economics and Statistics* (2024): 1–24.

75. N. Bloom, R. Han, and J. Liang, "Hybrid Working from Home Improves Retention without Damaging Performance," *Nature* 630 (2024): 920–925, https://doi.org/10.1038/s41586-024-07500-2.

Index

agglomeration economics, 129
agriculture, 39
AI. *See* artificial intelligence (AI)
airports, 39
alignment, in transitioning to WFA, 113, 114, 116–118
Allen, Thomas J., 57
all-remote arrangement
  definition of, 9, 23
  global talent access and, 22–24
Almeida, Paul, 130
Amabile, Teresa, 62
American Bar Association, 86–87
Amrith, Sunil, 148
Apple, 32, 55, 57
artificial intelligence (AI), 3, 4
asynchronous communication, 57–61
  benefits and challenges of, 61–64
  best practices for, 64–66
  knowledge sharing and, 68–69
  in transitioning to WFA, 116–118
automation, 3, 4, 37, 40, 41, 49
Ayoubi, Charles, 94–95
Azure, 43

Bahar, Dany, 94, 136
Bena, Jan, 23–24
benefits, 37, 120
  national/regional policies and, 43–46
  relocation and, 144
biases
  combating, 99–100
  isolation and, 98–99
  managerial, isolation and, 82–84
Bloom, Nicholas, 30–31, 82, 153
blue-collar workers, 40–42
BMW, 39–40
Bojinov, Iavor, 84, 89
BRAC, 16, 151–153
brain drain, 4, 33–35, 120
brainstorming, 61–62, 66
brainwriting, 62, 66
burnout, 81, 86–87, 99–102
business case, 6, 15–35
  cost savings and, 31–32
  global talent access and, 22–26
  societal benefits and, 32–35
  worker productivity and, 26–31
business trips, 16, 93–94

career development, 31
  isolation and, 81–84
  quarterly hybrid arrangement and, 110
  traditional relocation and, 129
Chattopadhyay, Shinjinee, 139
Chauvin, Jasmina, 69
Cisco, 48–49
climate change, 148–150
Codi, 117

codification of knowledge, 70–79, 113
benefits and challenges of, 72–73
best practices for, 73–79
monthly hybrid approach and, 108, 115
quarterly hybrid approach and, 116
in transitioning to WFA, 116–118
weekly hybrid approach and, 114
Cohli, Hari P., 133
collaboration, 62, 67
company offsites and, 93–94
collegiality, 85–86
colocation, constrained, 94–97
commitment, 85, 87–88
to organizational change, 118
quarterly hybrid arrangement and, 110
communication, 4, 6, 31, 53–54, 55–66, 153
asynchronous, 57–61
benefits and challenges of asynchronous, 61–64
best practices for, 64–66
collaboration and, 93–94
company offsites and, 94–95
at GitLab, 58–60, 75–76
hybrid approaches and, 114, 115
knowledge sharing and, 67–79
miscommunication in, 56
monthly hybrid approach and, 108
setting aside time for, 69–70
spontaneity in, 55–56, 57, 87–90
virtual vs. in-person, 82
virtual watercoolers and, 87–90
communities, 16, 120
relocation and, 146–148
societal benefits and, 32–35
commute time/distance, 9, 13, 18–20, 33, 35, 120
economic/environmental friction and, 148–149
hybrid work and, 105–106, 117, 151
company offsites, 90–99
fighting bias in, 99–100
monthly hybrid approach and, 107
quarterly hybrid approach and, 115–116
contextual knowledge, 131–136
contract workers, 45–46
Cook, Tim, 55
costs, 16
of moving, 148, 149
real estate and lease, 23–24, 106
savings with WFA, 31–32
Covid-19 pandemic, 1, 17–18, 64, 119, 127
isolation and, 83
overwork and burnout in, 86–87
relocation and, 141
weekly hybrid approach after, 105
creativity, 61–63
geographic mobility and, 135
cultural distance, 146, 147–148
culture, organizational, 84–87
company offsites and, 91

daylight saving time, 69
digital nomads, 6, 37, 46–49
tax policies and, 46
village for, 49
visas for, 6, 25, 38, 46–48, 96, 123–125
digital twins, 3, 6, 37–43, 119
Dimon, Jamie, 82

distributed work, 87, 91, 99, 110, 118–120
definition of, 9
diversity, 22–26
isolation and, 99–100
documentation, 71–73, 77–79. *See also* codification of knowledge
Doist, 16, 22–23
communication at, 60–61, 65
donut effect, 21–22
dopamine, 63, 65
downtime, 92–93
downtown areas, 21–22
Dutch East India Company, 56

economic frictions, 141, 148–150
Economic Report of the President of the United States, 3
Elkins, Caroline, 148
Emanuel, Natalia, 31
Employer of Record (EOR), 45
Enerjisa Üretim, 40, 42–43
engagement, 63–64
entrepreneurship, 137, 140
environmental issues, 33, 120
relocation and, 141, 148–150
European Union, 44
eXp, 16, 22, 23–24
experimentation, 111–113

familial obligations, 146
Fang, Tommy Pan, 69
Fayard, Anne-Laure, 62
feedback, asynchronous communication and, 59
financial capital, 130, 136–138
flexibility, 2, 119–120
balancing isolation and, 7–8
hybrid work and, 104
monthly hybrid approach and, 107–108
productivity and, 30–31, 151–153
worker preference for, 151–153
Florida, Richard, 129
foreign direct investment, 137–138
Foster, Wade, 23, 93

geographic immobility, 141
geographic mobility, 7–8, 15, 17–22. *See also* relocation model, traditional
monthly hybrid approach and, 107–108
place of residence determination and, 44–45
quality of life and, 28–30
quarterly hybrid arrangement and, 109
worker issues with, 25
GitLab, 16, 20–21, 22–23, 28
communication at, 58–60, 75–76
cost savings at, 32
knowledge codification at, 74–76
knowledge sharing at, 68–69
Glaeser, Edward, 129
Global Talent Stream, 25
Global Workplace Analytics, 32
Goldman Sachs, 84–85, 86, 87
Google, 48
Grohsjean, Thorsten, 76–77
Gupta, Arpit, 21–22

Haas, Martine, 71, 73
hackathons, 92
Hansen, Morten, 71, 73
Harrington, Emma, 31
Harvard Business School, 57
health care, 39, 101

health insurance, 46, 145
Henderson, Rebecca, 130
Hinds, Pamela J., 88
Ho, Lisa, 26
homesickness, 146–147
homophily, 98–99
hoteling, 108
Hsu, David H., 22
hukou system, China, 142–143
Hunt, Jennifer, 139
hybrid work arrangements, 2
  definition of, 9
  frequency of in-person days in, 104–105
  isolation and, 82–83
  monthly, 107–109
  pace of transitioning from, 110–113
  popularity of, 7–8, 151–153
  prevalence of, 7, 103, 105
  processes for, 116–118
  quarterly, 109–110, 111–112, 113
  stages in transitioning from, 104–110
  traditional, 20
  transition to WFA from, 7, 103–118
  venue of in-person days in, 104–105
  weekly, 105–107

IBM, 32
identity, shared, 98–99
implementation, 4
incentives
  for combating bias, 100
  for digital nomads, 38, 47
  for knowledge codification, 73, 77–78
  for relocation, 149, 150
information costs, 148
information spillover, 130
innovation, 55–56
  asynchronous communication and, 61–63
  colocation and, 95–97
  company offsites and, 93–94
  geographic mobility and, 131–136
in-person work, 20
  definition of, 9
  processes for hybrid arrangements and, 116–118
  transitioning from hybrid to WFA, 104–105
INSEAD, 88
insurance networks, 146
introverts, 62
isolation, 4, 7, 31, 53–54
  balancing flexibility and, 7–8
  company offsites and, 90–99
  hybrid work and, 104
  productivity and, 151–153
  professional, 81–84
  quarterly hybrid arrangement and, 110
  social, 81, 84–87
  socialization, burnout, and, 99–102
  solving, 87–99
  virtual watercoolers and, 87–90, 97–99

Jaffe, Adam B., 130
Jalota, Suhani, 26
Jang, Sujin, 94–95
Jeon, So Hee, 83–84
job satisfaction, 22, 83, 152, 153

JPMorgan Chase, 82
Jupyter Notebook, 43

Kerr, William, 25, 143–144
Khanna, Tarun, 148, 151–153
Kim, Do Yoon, 94, 131–134
knowledge sharing, 4, 6–7, 53–54, 67–79
  knowledge codification and, 69–79
  traditional relocation model and, 130–136
Kogut, Bruce, 130
Koo, Wesley W., 94
Kown, Myungjung, 83–84
Kulchina, Elena, 140

Lane, Jacqueline, 84, 89
language issues, 147–148
leaders and leadership, 4, 118
learning. *See also* knowledge sharing
  social, 68
  vicarious, 68
licensing issues, 25, 144–145
Lim, Chaeyoon, 91
LinkedIn, 26

machine learning, 3
Makridis, Christos, 151–153
managers and management, 2–3, 4, 6–7, 120
  isolation and, 81
  location requirements and, 17–19
  monthly hybrid approach and, 108
  performance ratings bias and, 83–84
  strategies for, 53–54
  transitioning to WFA and, 113–116
manufacturing, 39, 41–42
Mark, Gloria, 64
Mater Private Hospital, Dublin, 39
meetings
  asynchronous communication and, 62–63
  virtual watercoolers and, 88–89
mentors and mentoring, 53, 81–84
  company offsites and, 90–97
  fighting bias in, 100
  similarity/diversity and, 98–99
  virtual watercoolers and, 89
Meta, 25–26, 106
Microsoft, 67
MobSquad, 16, 25, 143–144
monthly hybrid arrangement, 107–109, 111
  best practices for, 114–115
  definition of, 9
Mortensen, Mark, 88
multinational corporations, 56–57, 129
Murph, Darren, 77

Nadella, Satya, 67
networks and networking, 64
  company offsites and, 90–97
  demographics and, 98
  fighting bias in, 100
  isolation and, 81–84
  relocation and, 139–140
  virtual watercoolers and, 87–90
  who to include in, 97–99
Nomad Village Brazil, 49
noncompete clauses, 145

norms, 53
  for asynchronous communication, 58–60, 64–66
  relocation and, 145
  traditional relocation model and, 130, 136–138

occupational frictions, 141, 144–145
office sharing, 108
ongoing presence, defining, 44–45
organizational frictions, 141, 144–145
overwork, 86–87, 101–102

permanent establishment, defining, 44–45
personal frictions, 141, 146–148
pharmaceutical industry, 131–134
pilot programs, 65–66
place of residence, determining, 44–45
policies and procedures
  benefits, 37
  implementation of, 35
  national and regional, 43–46
  relocation and, 141, 145
  social welfare, 37
  taxation, 37
  transitioning to WFA and, 110–113
productivity, 26–31, 119–120
  burnout and, 100–102
  effects of flexibility and isolation on, 151–153
  monthly hybrid approach and, 108
  organizational commitment and, 85
  promotions and, 82–84
  quality metrics and, 101
  quarterly hybrid arrangement and, 110
  in transitioning to WFA, 116–118
Professional Employer Organization (PEO), 45
profitability, 26–31
Puranam, Phanish, 181

quality, 61
  in knowledge codification, 77, 78–79
quality of life, 28–30, 119–120
  asynchronous communication and, 62–63, 65
  boundaries and, 65
quarterly hybrid arrangement, 109–110, 111
  best practices for, 115–116
  definition of, 9

Radious, 117
Ramanujan, Srinivasa, 148
Rapoport, Hillel, 136
Rawji, Irfhan, 143–144
real estate costs, 23–24, 148
  hybrid models and, 106
  monthly hybrid approach and, 107–108
  quarterly hybrid arrangement and, 110
  worker quality of life and, 28–30
recruitment and hiring, 16, 21, 120–121
  global, 22–26
regulatory frictions, 141–144
relocation model, traditional, 7–8, 15, 25, 127–153
  challenges of, 141–150

knowledge transfer/ recombination and, 130–136
opportunities for individuals and, 130, 138–140
regulatory frictions in, 141–144
social capital, financial capital, organizational norms, and, 136–138
value of, 128–130
WFA as alternative to, 150
remote-first arrangement, 9, 57
remote work. *See also* work from anywhere (WFA)
accessing global talent through, 22–24
definition of, 1, 9
geographic flexibility and, 17–19
productivity and, 31
worker preference for, 21, 119
reporting, 63–64
resistance, 5
retention rates, 28
return-to-office (RTO) mandates, 21–22
rituals, at company offsites, 91, 115–116
ROPE framework, 141–150

salaries/income
geographic differences and, 28–30
relocation and, 139–140
Salihefendic, Amir, 23, 97
Saxenian, AnnaLee, 135
Schirmann, Kyle, 151–153
sensors, 4
Sercomm, 143
Sevcenko, Victoria, 94–95
Shea, Nicolás, 95–96
Siemens, 39
Sijbrandij, Sid, 23, 75
skills training
digital twins and, 40, 42–43
relocation and, 139
Skinner, B. F., 63
sky-blue-collared workers, 40–42
Slack, 63, 94–95
social capital, 130, 136–138
socialization, 99–102
societal benefits, 32–35
software as a service (SaaS), 20–21
Solomon, David, 84–85, 86
special-team approach, 74, 78–79
split mobility decisions, 149–150
Starr, Evan, 29, 34
Start-Up Chile, 95–97
Startup Madeira, 49
stigmergy, 76–77
Subramaniam, N. G., 24–25
Sun Microsystems, 32

talent attraction programs, 33–35, 47–48
talent pools, 2–3, 5, 6. *See also* digital nomads
accessing diverse global, 22–26
benefits of WFA for, 21–22
hybrid models and, 106
spatial distribution of, 46–49
Tambe, Prasanna B., 22
"tap the shoulder" approach, 71–72
Tata Consultancy Services (TCS), 16, 24–25
TCS. *See* Tata Consultancy Services (TCS)
Teach for America, 34
teams
company offsites and, 90–97
hybrid models and, 106–107

teams (*continued*)
  transitioning from hybrid to WFA in, 104–105
  transition pace and, 110–113
Teams, 56, 63
technology, 4
  digital twins, 3, 6, 37–43, 119
  WFA boundaries expanded by, 3, 4, 37–43
telecommuting, at USPTO, 26–30
Teodorovicz, Thomaz, 29, 34
terminology, 9
time and time zone issues, 19, 56–57
  knowledge sharing, 67–68
Time magazine, 21
Todoist, 97
Trajtenberg, Manuel, 130
trends, emerging, 6, 37–49
  digital twins, 37–43
truth, knowledge codification and, 73
Tulsa Remote, 16, 29, 34–35, 47
turmeric, 133
turnover, 16, 28–31
Twist, 60–61, 97

Unilever, 41–42, 43
United States Patent and Trademark Office, 3–4, 16, 24–26
  cost savings at, 32
  organizational attachment at, 85
  pollution reduction from WFA at, 33
  productivity at, 26–30
USPTO. *See* United States Patent and Trademark Office

values, company, 85, 87–88
Venywhere, 48–49
video messaging/conferencing, 56, 58
  virtual watercoolers and, 88–89
virtual watercoolers, 87–90, 97–99
  fighting bias in, 99–100
  monthly hybrid approach and, 108, 115
  quarterly hybrid approach and, 115–116
  in transitioning to WFA, 116–118
visas
  digital nomad, 6, 25, 38, 46–48, 96, 123–125
  regulatory frictions around, 143–144

Wahba, Jackline, 137
watercooler effect, 55–56
watercoolers, virtual, 87–90
weekly hybrid arrangement, 105–107, 111
  definition of, 9
  management best practices for, 113–114
wellness, 115, 116, 117, 120
wellness teams, 101
WFA. *See* work from anywhere (WFA)
whole-team approach, 74
Wikipedia, 76
women, access to work for, 26
workcations, 48–49
work environments, worker power over, 17–20
workflow, 63–64
work from anywhere (WFA)
  analytical framework for, 111–112
  business case for, 6, 15–35
  definition of, 1–2, 9, 17–22
  digital nomads and, 6
  digital twins and, 6

emerging trends in, 6, 37–49
future of the workplace and, 119–121
management strategies for, 53–54
research on, 3–5, 7–8
strategic importance of, 13
transitioning to, 7, 103–118, 120–121
what workers love about it, 2
as win-win strategy, 2–3, 16, 119–120
worker preference for, 21
work from home (WFH), 2, 13
definition of, 9
geographic mobility and, 18–19
transition to WFA from, 7, 103–118
at USPTO, 26–28
work hours, 61
work-life balance, 54, 62–63, 152–153
knowledge sharing and, 69–70
writing, 65

Y Combinator, 95
Young, Cristobal, 91

Zapier, 16, 22–23
company retreats at, 92–93
homophily at, 98
quarterly hybrid arrangement at, 109
Zenou, Yves, 137
Zoom, 56, 65, 82, 106
virtual watercoolers and, 88–89

Acknowledgments

I would like to acknowledge my debt to all my research colleagues, doctoral students, and mentors over the years, especially Rajshree Agarwal, Gautam Ahuja, Dany Bahar, Nicholas Bloom, Jasmina Chauvin, Kirk Doran, Alfonso Gambardella, Ina Ganguli, Britta Glennon, Zeke Hernandez, Pamela Hinds, David Hsu, William Kerr, Tarun Khanna, Do Yoon Kim, Wesley Koo, David Kryscynski, Elena Kulchina, Barbara Larson, Megan Lawrence, Anita McGahan, Astrid Marinoni, Chris Marquis, Lamar Pierce, Henning Piezunka, Phanish Puranam, Victoria Sevcenko, Jasjit Singh, Evan Starr, Thomaz Teodorovicz, and Dan Wang. I am also indebted to the brilliant minds in the business world from whom I have a learned a lot, including Annie Dean, Brian Elliott, Wade Foster, Drew Hirshfeld, Carly Moulton, Darren Murph, Irfhan Rawji, Sid Sijbrandij, and Ben Stewart. Finally, my thanks to Rebecca Hinds for helping to draft a subsection of the book, Emma Salomon for her support during preparation of early drafts, and Emma Waldman, who helped shape the book with her excellent editorial suggestions.

About the Author

PRITHWIRAJ (RAJ) CHOUDHURY is a globally recognized expert on the future of work. Serving on the faculties at Wharton and Harvard Business School for over a decade, he studies the changing geography of work. His research focuses on management practices that support hybrid work, remote work, and work from anywhere (WFA); how companies, communities, and countries are competing for remote workers; and how AI and automation can help both desk workers and deskless workers work from anywhere. In 2023, *Forbes* included him in their Future of Work 50 list, and in 2024 he was included in the *Time*-Charter 30 list of thought leaders shaping the future of work. He previously worked at McKinsey & Company and Microsoft and obtained his doctorate from Harvard. His research has been cited by the BBC, CNBC, *New York Times, Wall Street Journal, Washington Post, Forbes, Fortune, Freakonomics, Al Jazeera, El País,* and *Times of India,* among other outlets. He has delivered keynotes and provided advice on the future of work to organizations as diverse as Atlassian, Google, ITC, Deel, Young Presidents' Organization, the Council on Foreign Relations, the British Parliament, and the United Nations.